I0756807

RWANDA'S STILLBORN
MIDDLE-INCOME ECONOMY

Paul Kagame, Bill Clinton, Tony Blair, Jim Yong Kim, the World Bank and Rwanda Vision 2020 Fiasco

DAVID HIMBARA

authorHOUSE

AuthorHouse™
1663 Liberty Drive
Bloomington, IN 47403
www.authorhouse.com
Phone: 1 (800) 839-8640

© 2020 David Himbara. All rights reserved.

No part of this book may be reproduced, stored in a retrieval system, or transmitted by any means without the written permission of the author.

Published by AuthorHouse 01/02/2020

ISBN: 978-1-7283-4144-6 (sc)
ISBN: 978-1-7283-4143-9 (hc)
ISBN: 978-1-7283-4142-2 (e)

Library of Congress Control Number: 2019921200

Print information available on the last page.

Any people depicted in stock imagery provided by Getty Images are models, and such images are being used for illustrative purposes only.
Certain stock imagery © Getty Images.

This book is printed on acid-free paper.

Because of the dynamic nature of the Internet, any web addresses or links contained in this book may have changed since publication and may no longer be valid. The views expressed in this work are solely those of the author and do not necessarily reflect the views of the publisher, and the publisher hereby disclaims any responsibility for them.

CONTENTS

TABLES

DEDICATION

To Rwandan teachers who toil under harsh conditions and yet are key to developing what Rwanda needs most—human capital.

I dedicate this book to Rwandan teachers. In 2008, without any warning or preparation, head of state Paul Kagame switched Rwanda's teaching language from French to English in his drive to join the Commonwealth. To deal with the chaos that followed, Kagame's government recruited hundreds of teachers from Uganda and Kenya to mentor and improve the teaching of English in primary and secondary schools in Rwanda. The scheme soon fell apart—the government had no money to sustain it. The government then scrapped the use of English for pre-primary and lower primary schools in 2015. And in December 2019, Kagame made a U-turn, reinstating English as the teaching language in pre-primary and lower primary schools. Twelve years since the initial debacle, Rwanda's education remains in shambles. As the World Bank explains, "The survival rate in basic education is low, reflecting high dropout rates; disparities by urban-rural residence and by household income are significant," while "learning outcomes are low by regional and international standards."[1] Similarly, the International Monetary Fund indicates that "Rwanda's annual public spending on education—at 3.6 percent of GDP—is lower than in other peer countries" and that "Rwanda spends only about 30 percent of its education budget on

---

[1] World Bank, "Rwanda Quality Basic Education for Human Capital Development Project (P168551)," July 9, 2019, http://documents.worldbank.org/curated/en/184411564797693303/pdf/Rwanda-Quality-Basic-Education-for-Human-Capital-Development-Project.pdf

teacher compensation vs. 45 percent in higher-performing comparable countries."[2] After two decades of pleading, Kagame finally raised teachers' salaries by 10 percent on January 28, 2019.[3] The salary increase, however, did not lift the teachers of Rwanda from poverty. With the 10 percent raise, a primary school teacher's monthly earnings increased from RWF44,000 or US$48 to RWF48,400 or US$53. This translates to US$1.76 a day, which is less than the international poverty line of US$1.90 a day. There can be no question that teachers are the unsung heroes in Rwandan lives—they do so much for so little in return. This is especially the case for women and men who teach in rural areas where most Rwandans live under appallingly poor conditions that have hardly changed in the past twenty years in which Kagame supposedly transformed Rwanda into a middle-income economy.

---

[2] IMF, Staff Report for The 2019 Article Iv Consultation and Request for A Three-Year Policy Coordination Instrument, July 2019, file:///C:/Users/David/Downloads/1RWAEA2019001%20(2).pdf

[3] Republic of Rwanda, "Statement on Cabinet Decisions of 28.01.2019," http://gov.rw/newsdetails2/?tx_ttnews%5Btt_news%5D=2093&cHash=593e3bce6910d301bb4c19d329a102c7

ABOUT THE AUTHOR

David Himbara is an educator, author, and professor of international development based in Toronto, Canada. From 1994, Himbara lived and worked in South Africa, where he was the lead consultant for teams that conducted the country's Ten-Year Development Review in 2004, among other projects. Himbara led the core team responsible for Knowledge Management Africa (KMA), which coached African governments in evidence-based policymaking. Himbara has taught at several universities in North America and Africa, including the University of Witwatersrand's Graduate School of Public and Development Management in South Africa, from 2010 to 2013. While there, Himbara led a team that succeeded in bringing the World Bank's Centre for Learning on Evaluation and Results (CLEAR) to the university, where the program supports governmental clients throughout sub-Saharan Africa. In 2011, Himbara served as a lead consultant for the African Development Bank, and in 2010, he served as chief strategist for the UN Development Programme (UNDP) in South Africa. Other major assignments included lead consultancy on trade and investment harmonization for the Southern African Community (SADC) and lead strategist on Indonesian export policy into South Africa.

A Rwandan-Canadian, Himbara spent six years working for Rwanda's President Paul Kagame. From 2000 to 2002, Himbara was the principal private secretary to the president. Himbara returned to Rwanda in 2006 after President Kagame asked him to lead socioeconomic reforms aimed at accelerating development. Tasked with improving national competitiveness, Himbara spearheaded efforts that ultimately improved

Rwanda's ranking in the World Bank's annual *Doing Business Report* from 143rd to 67th out of 183 countries; Rwanda was named top reformer by the 2010 *Doing Business Report*. In this phase, Himbara set up and headed the Strategy and Policy Unit, Office of the President. In this capacity, he led the establishment of the Rwanda Development Board (RDB) and was its founding chairperson. In addition, Himbara was the chairperson of the World Bank-funded Human and Institutional Development Agency (HIDA).

Before his time in Rwanda, Himbara also lectured on economic development as a senior lecturer at the University of Witwatersrand from 1994 to 1997 and was an assistant professor at Southern University in Louisiana, USA, from 1991 to 1993. He taught international development at Centennial College, Toronto, Canada, from 2015-2019.

Himbara completed his PhD in political economy at Queen's University in Kingston, Ontario, Canada, in 1991. He is widely published on social and economic development in leading journals and online. Himbara's dissertation on the role of domestic entrepreneurs and the state in socioeconomic transformation was published as a book in 1994: *Kenyan Capitalists, the State, and Development*. Among his more recent books is *Kagame's Economic Mirage*, published in 2016.

PREFACE

During the two tenures I worked for Rwandan head of state, Paul Kagame, fellow senior staff and I persistently faced a difficult situation. On the one hand, reforming government for improved delivery meant we needed to conduct needs assessments to fix the gaps or weaknesses. On the other hand, President Kagame wanted to show that he had already transformed Rwanda into an African and even a global success story. It was in these circumstances that Kagame assembled a diehard support network of global influencers who championed him as an African visionary leader. Most prominent of Kagame's global team includes former US President Bill Clinton, former British Prime Minister Tony Blair, former World Bank President Jim Yong Kim, and the World Bank itself.

Long after I left Rwanda, I saw how Kagame's endeavor of marketing his purported social and economic successes firmly became part of his global network's language. In speeches and writings, Kagame, Clinton, Blair, Kim, and the World Bank similarly described Rwanda in a disconcerting manner. They claimed that Rwanda was among the world's best led and most friendly country to investment, ranking ahead of such countries as Japan in the ease of doing business. Rwanda's healthcare system would soon become a model for the world. With the help of the World Bank, Kagame launched successor development plans to Vision 2020, aiming to turn Rwanda into an upper-middle-income economy by 2035 and a high-income economy by 2050. This is odd as Rwanda was not even close to lifting itself from the ranks of the world's poorest among low-income economies.

When I initially thought of writing this book, I wanted to give it a speaking-from-the-heart style that would be easily accessible, free of jargon, and free of cumbersome footnotes. But I had to modify my approach. Extensive references were unavoidable because Rwanda's story, as officially narrated, has gained wide but mistaken acceptance. To properly dispel Paul Kagame's delusional grandeur, I needed to support my argument with evidence, which meant references and long quotes from a variety of sources, especially the Rwandan government. This is the only viable method for successfully countering official propaganda. The Rwandan government's own data and official documents sharply contradict Kagame's inflated claims.

I have also extensively used data from the World Bank and the International Monetary Fund (IMF). As a development scholar and practitioner, I take this opportunity to pay tribute to the former president of the World Bank Group, Robert Zoellick, under whose leadership the World Bank formalized its practice of making research and knowledge freely available to all of us. As Zoellick explained, "Knowledge is power. Making our knowledge widely and readily available will empower others to come up with solutions to the world's toughest problems. Our new Open Access policy is the natural evolution for a World Bank that is opening up more and more."[4] The IMF is equally generous—it grants a "fair use" of its materials to academics, journalists, and other interested parties for purposes "such as criticism, comment, news reporting, teaching, scholarship, or research."[5] Together with the government's own data, the World Bank's and IMF's statistics and analyses compensate for lack of domestic social and economic research due to repression that renders critical writings a crime in Kagame's Rwanda.

---

[4] World Bank, "World Bank Announces Open Access Policy for Research and Knowledge, Launches Open Knowledge Repository", April 10, 2012, https://www.worldbank.org/en/news/press-release/2012/04/10/world-bank-announces-open-access-policy-for-research-and-knowledge-launches-open-knowledge-repository

[5] IMF, "Copyright and Usage," https://www.imf.org/external/terms.htm

Paul Kagame assembled a powerful global lobby, led by former US president Bill Clinton, former British prime minister Tony Blair, former World Bank president Jim Yong Kim to champion his Vision 2020. These men proclaimed Kagame a visionary leader and sought to assist him to transform Rwanda into a middle-income economy by 2020. Clinton's Clinton Health Access Initiative (CHAI) and Partners In Health (PIH), co-founded by Jim Yong Kim and Paul Farmer, would build in Rwanda a global healthcare system model. Blair's objective was to reinforce the capacity of the Rwandan state and promote foreign investment. Supported by Clinton, Kagame, and Farmer, among others, Kim became the president of the World Bank in 2012. Until Kim's resignation in January 2019, the World Bank became Rwanda's largest financier and praise-singer. By then, Kagame had proclaimed Rwanda an African economic lion, while the World Bank assisted Rwanda to map the way forward into becoming an upper-middle-income economy by 2035 and a high-income economy by 2050—as if the lower-middle-income economy was already a reality.

My main argument in this book is that the Kagame-Clinton-Blair-Kim-World Bank narrative of turning Rwanda into a middle-income economy by 2020 is bogus. Rwanda Vision 2020 was a total failure in each of the stated objectives, namely, "the efficient state, skilled human capital, vibrant private sector, world class physical infrastructure and modern agriculture and livestock, all geared towards prospering in national, regional and global markets" and a per capita income of

US$1,240.[6] According to the International Monetary Fund, Rwanda's per capita income was US$786 in 2018, and is projected to reach US$873 in 2020, and US$1,140 in 2024.[7] If one uses the lower middle-income international poverty line set at $3.20 a day, 80 percent of Rwandans remain poor.[8] Rwanda's human capital development is another disaster. Rwanda's human capital index is below the average of sub-Saharan African and low-income economies.[9] And Rwanda's economy is essentially driven by the public sector, while the private sector has yet to takeoff. As for Rwanda's integration into international markets, a 2019 World Bank report indicated that "the importance of exports has increased ever so slightly, from 1.8% in 1995 to 2.0% in 2015, but remains much lower than in the rest of sub-Saharan Africa where exports account on average for 11 percent." The report concludes that "the overall integration of Rwanda in global value chains remains very limited."[10]

Kagame deserves a medal for a different reason—he is a master of false branding in a double sense. First, he succeeded spectacularly in marketing his delusional grandeur of transforming a subsistence economy into a middle-income state in a single generation. Second, he understood that prominent politicians such as Clinton and Blair seek to remain globally relevant after they leave office and need poor countries such as Rwanda to promote their international charities, deliver speeches about helping poor people, and make money. Kagame

---

[6] Republic of Rwanda, "Rwanda Vision 2020" revised in 2012, http://www.minecofin.gov.rw/fileadmin/templates/documents/NDPR/Vision_2020_.pdf

[7] IMF, "GDP per capita, current prices," https://www.imf.org/external/datamapper/NGDPDPC@WEO/OEMDC/ADVEC/WEOWORLD

[8] World Bank, "Poverty headcount ratio at US$3.20 a day," https://data.worldbank.org/indicator/SI.POV.LMIC?locations=MA&most_recent_value_desc=true

[9] World Bank, "Rwanda Human Capital Index," 2017, https://databank.worldbank.org/data/download/hci/HCI_2pager_RWA.pdf

[10] Garth Frazer and Johannes Van Biesebroeck, *The Extent of Engagement in Global Value Chains by Firms in Rwanda*, World Bank Policy Research Working Paper 8979, August 2019, http://documents.worldbank.org/curated/en/617871565698066427/pdf/The-Extent-of-Engagement-in-Global-Value-Chains-by-Firms-in-Rwanda.pdf

happily gave them the platform in return for championing his false cause. Self-interest equally drove Kagame and his ruling party, which, instead of promoting the country's private sector, built a business empire that became Rwanda's largest investment group that thrives on state capture and cronyism.

This book has twelve chapters. In chapter 1, I illustrate how Rwanda's middle-income economy was stillborn. In chapter 2, I present Kagame's global marketing of his delusion of grandeur and how he opportunistically formed his coalition of high-level influencers and donors to champion his visionary leadership and his Vision 2020. In chapter 3, I illustrate in greater detail, Rwanda's middle-income economy fiasco using quantitative and qualitative data from mainly the Rwandan government and the World Bank. Chapter 4 shows how foreign-aid donors moved the goalposts, resorting to calling Rwanda "an impressive economic performer but poor country" on realizing that Rwanda's middle-income economy is a mirage. Chapter 5 illustrates the fantasy of building a global healthcare model in Rwanda. I also review the infamous diversion of US$150 million of American foreign aid to Rwanda by the Mrs. Hillary Clinton-led US State Department to Rwanda-based health charities associated with Bill Clinton, Paul Farmer and Jim Yong Kim. Chapter 6 reviews Blair's attempts at reinforcing the capacity of the Rwanda state while promoting foreign investment. Highlighted is also the role of Tony Blair's wife, Cherie Blair in providing legal support to the Kagame government, not least how Mrs. Blair kept a Rwandan military general accused of human rights abuses out of British and Spanish jails. Chapter 7 examines how Kagame built a US$500 million business empire for his ruling party that benefits from state capture and cronyism, which effectively quashed the imperative of creating a private sector-led economy in Rwanda. Chapter 8 probes where the US$20.8 billion aid money, purportedly pumped into Rwanda from 1994 to 2020, went. Chapter 9 takes a closer look at the US$200 million World Bank loan to Rwanda approved in 2018 on the eve of Jim Yong Kim's departure from the bank. The larger part of this loan was earmarked for building 11,000 classrooms and

14,680 latrines as a means of improving Rwanda's human capital. A middle-income economy receiving foreign aid to build latrines is rather odd. Even more astonishing is how Kagame became the champion of human capital development in Jim Yong Kim's World Bank. Chapter 10 looks at the Kagame's closure of the common border with Uganda through which most of Rwanda's US$3 billion annual international trade transits. The chapter also reviews the US's suspension of Rwanda from trade facilitation. The concluding chapter reflects on the failure of Kagame's Faustian bargain.

CHAPTER 1

Rwanda's Stillborn Middle-Income Economy and Kagame's Faustian Bargain

In 2013, seven years before Rwanda was to complete the projected timeline to become a middle-income economy, the Rwandan head of state, Paul Kagame, declared the mission accomplished. He announced that he had transformed Rwanda into an African economic lion, inspired by the Asian tigers of South Korea, Singapore, Hong Kong, and Taiwan. As he put it, "We have decentralized the state, reformed our business sector and strengthened our institutions. But we have also invested in health care, agriculture and education. As a result, the World Bank this year ranked Rwanda as the eighth easiest place in the world to start a business." Kagame added that "in our pursuit of progress, we have of course looked to East Asia's so-called 'tiger' economies for inspiration."[11] On September 14, 2019, Kagame asserted that Rwanda was the world's most impressive economic performer. He proclaimed that in 2018, Rwanda's economy grew by 8.6 percent, adding that the results in 2019 were more spectacular and inclusive than anywhere else in the world: "In some cases, such growth only benefits a minority, but in our case, the growth benefited the majority." In the first quarter of

---

[11] Paul Kagame, "Rwanda and the new lions of Africa," Wall Street Journal, May 19, 2013, https://www.wsj.com/articles/SB10001424127887324767004578485234 078541160

2019, according to Kagame, the growth rate was 8.4 percent, while in the second quarter, the economy grew by 12.2 percent. He concluded that "few countries anywhere in the world can achieve these remarkable results."[12] And on December 20, 2019, Kagame declared Rwandan economic performance "an unequalled record."[13]

Prominent members of the global elites, led by Clinton, Blair, and Jim Yong Kim, had already jumped on Kagame's bandwagon, proclaiming him a visionary leader who was turning Rwanda into a prosperous nation. The Clinton Health Access Initiative (CHAI)[14] and Partners In Health (PIH),[15] cofounded by Jim Yong Kim and Paul Farmer, set up health charities in Rwanda starting in the 2000s to build what they termed a global health-care system model. Blair launched his Tony Blair Africa Governance Initiative in Rwanda "to make government work."[16] The World Bank became a staunch believer in Kagame's Rwanda, regularly awarding it accolades and ranking it the best-managed state not only in Africa but globally;[17] twenty-ninth of 190 best countries for doing business, ahead of such economies as Japan, Switzerland, and China;[18] and the third-fastest growing economy

---

[12] President Paul Kagame, "Remarks by RPF Chairman Paul Kagame," September 14, 2019, https://youtu.be/904D9w8kiPU

[13] Paul Kagame, State of The Nation Address 17th Umushyikirano, December 19, 2019, https://twitter.com/UrugwiroVillage/status/1207626768657657857

[14] Clinton Health Assess Initiative, retrieved September 7, 2019, https://clintonhealthaccess.org/

[15] Partners In Health, "Rwanda: A Model for Building Health Systems," retrieved September 7, 2019, https://www.pih.org/country/rwanda

[16] Tony Blair Africa Governance Initiative, "Our mission is to make government work for the world's poorest people," retrieved September 7, 2019, http://www.africagovernance.org/

[17] World Bank, "Understanding the Africa country policy and institutional assessment (CPIA) 2017, September 12, 2018, https://www.worldbank.org/en/region/afr/publication/in-five-charts-understanding-the-africa-country-policy-and-institutional-assessment-cpia-report-for-2017,

[18] World Bank, "Doing Business 2019," May 19, 2019, https://www.worldbank.org/content/dam/doingBusiness/media/Annual-Reports/English/DB2019-report web-version.pdf

in the world.[19] The World Bank even went so far as to join forces with the Kagame government to craft successor strategies to Vision 2020 with the aim of propelling Rwanda into upper middle-income by 2035 and to high income by 2050. In other words, for Kagame and his staunch supporters, Rwanda was *already* speeding towards even greater prosperity.

But the Rwanda described by Kagame and his global network does not exist. Their version of Rwanda is a charade. The objectives of Vision 2020 were not achieved. An economy led by a responsive state, a dynamic private sector, robust human capital, and world-class infrastructure connecting Rwanda to regional and global markets did not materialize. To be sure, Kagame built mammoth infrastructures with the goal of creating new economic niches such as conference tourism. Towards that end, Kagame invested heavily into the national airline, RwandAir, Kigali Convention Centre (KCC), Kigali Basketball Arena, and sponsorship of European football clubs as a means of attracting tourists. Between RwandAir[20] and KCC,[21] Kagame spent at least US$1.4 billion between 2013 and 2016 which has created a significant debt burden. On top of the US$1.4 billion spent on RwandAir and Kigali Convention Centre, Kagame evidently added another US$1.3 billion to build a new international airport. On December 9, 2019, Rwanda and Qatar Airways signed an investment partnership for building Rwanda's new international airport, with the latter taking

---

[19] World Bank, GDP annual growth rates (%), 2018 https://data.worldbank.org/indicator/ny.gdp.mktp.kd.zg?most_recent_value_desc=true

[20] David Himbara, "RwandAir Bankrupting Rwanda – Open Letter to Presidents Yoweri Museveni and John Magufuli," Medium.com, May 17, 2018, https://medium.com/@david.himbara_27884/rwandair-bankrupting-rwanda-db766fc603ac

[21] Republic of Rwanda, Ministry of Finance and Economic Planning, "Rwanda's $400 million Eurobond named 2013 Deal of the Year by Euromoney, February 25, 2014, http://www.minecofin.gov.rw/index.php?id=12&tx_ttnews%5Btt_news%5D=161&cHash=84cafde2e62af961ff9b79a93e82f7f9

a 60 percent stake or US$780 million.[22] This means that Rwanda is responsible for 40 percent of the cost or US$520 million. It was not clear how the Kagame government would raise the money to finance its share of US$1.3 billion.

RwandAir debts had already prompted the IMF to state that Rwanda had breached a new external debt ceiling of US$500 million by US$87 million in 2018 and that the government proposed "to raise the indicative ceiling to US$800 million to accommodate this and potential other leases to replace existing aircraft."[23] Rwanda is once again in serious debt after receiving a debt relief package of about US$810 million in debt service back in 2000, which was "equal to US$452 million in net present value (NPV) terms."[24] By 2019, the Rwandan government's gross debt as a percent of GDP stood at 50 percent.[25]

The benefits of these major projects remain questionable. These projects are funded and executed by the public sector and have not stimulated the private sector which is by far the biggest failure in the past twenty years. Rwanda's tradable economy remains tiny. Over 99.3 percent of Rwanda's private-sector operations remain small and micro with dismal off-farm employability. These small and micro businesses

---

[22] Rwanda Development Board, "The Government of Rwanda and Qatar Airways today signed an investment partnership for Rwanda's new international airport," December 9, 2019, https://www.facebook.com/189020131134486/posts/2551797144856761?d=n&sfns=mo

[23] IMF, "RWANDA Ninth Review Under the Policy Support Instrument," May 23, 2018, file:///C:/Users/David/Downloads/cr18167.pdf

[24] IMF, "Rwanda to Receive US$810 Million in Debt Service Relief: The IMF and World Bank Support Debt Relief for Rwanda Under the Enhanced HIPC Initiative," December 22, 2000, https://www.imf.org/en/News/Articles/2015/09/14/01/49/pr0084

[25] IMF, "Rwanda – General government gross debt (Percent of GDP)," 2019, retrieved September 7, 2019, https://www.imf.org/external/datamapper/GGXWDG_NGDP@WEO/OEMDC/ADVEC/WEOWORLD

have an annual turnover of US$21,900 or less.[26] A World Bank study dated August 2019 indicated that there are 101 exporters in Rwanda but this includes "firms selling a mere US$10,000 per year", leading the Bank to conclude that "remarkably few firms in Rwanda are globally engaged. Even though the number of exporters increased over the last decade, especially among manufacturing firms, the total number of exporters remains extremely very low."[27]

With regards to human resources, Rwanda is in the bottom quantile of 157 countries and below the African and low-income countries' averages in the human capital index.[28] Basic life necessities such as food security remain a daily struggle for the people of Rwanda. Food insecurity affects almost 20 percent of the population but inflicts an even greater misery in rural areas especially in Rwandan districts such as Rutsiro where 49 percent suffer food insecurity versus 41 percent at Ngororero and 33 percent in Kayonza.[29] Chronic malnutrition is pervasive in Rwanda, with stunting levels in rural areas reaching nearly 50 percent.[30] Energy poverty also remains high. Some 99.6 percent of

---

[26] Republic of Rwanda, Rwanda Revenue Authority, "Annual Activity Report 2017/18," October 2018, https://www.rra.gov.rw/fileadmin/user_upload/rra_annual_activity_report_2017-18.pdf

[27] Garth Frazer and Johannes Biesebroeck, *The Extent of Engagement in Global Value Chains by Firms in Rwanda*, Op. Cit.

[28] World Bank, "Human Capital Index: Country Briefs and Data," 2018, https://www.worldbank.org/en/publication/human-capital

[29] World Bank, Rwanda Stunting Prevention and Reduction Project, "Restructuring Paper On A Proposed Project Restructuring Of Rwanda Stunting Prevention And Reduction Project Approved On February 28, 2018 To Ministry Of Finance And Economic Planning," February 28, 2018, http://documents.worldbank.org/curated/en/133331566305034640/pdf/Disclosable-Restructuring-Paper-Rwanda-Stunting-Prevention-and-Reduction-Project-P164845.pdf

[30] World Bank, Rwanda Economic Update, "Tackling Stunting: An Unfinished Agenda," June 2018, http://documents.worldbank.org/curated/en/360651529100512847/pdf/127256-NWP-P164510-PUBLIC-Rwanda-Economic-Update-ed-no-12-June-2018.pdf

Rwandan households cook with biomass,[31] while 31 percent of Rwanda's population is connected to grid electricity, and only 16 percent of the rural population has access to electricity.[32] Dependency on biomass for cooking has, in fact, increased since 2002. In the joint 2002 World Bank–International Monetary Fund assessment of Rwanda's poverty-reduction strategy, it was indicated that "for cooking, 98 percent of households rely on wood or charcoal. Electricity is used by 1 percent of urban households, and 0 percent of rural households. … For lighting, electricity is used by 39 percent of urban households and 1 percent of rural ones."[33] Put another way, since 2002, dependency on wood and charcoal for cooking *increased* by 1.6 percent.

The fiasco of the private sector, human capital, infrastructure, and the misallocation of public finances by an opaque state explain why Rwanda remains very poor. As noted earlier, 80 percent of Rwandans are poor as per the international poverty line of US$3.20 a day, an indicator that is used to measure poverty in lower middle-income economies. But even at the international poverty line of US$1.90 a day, which is used to measure poverty in low-income countries, 55.5 percent of Rwandans are poor. This makes Rwanda the poorest country in the East African Community (EAC), except for conflict-affected Burundi.[34] The World Bank alerts us, however, that poverty "soars to 76 percent for

---

[31] World Bank, "RWANDA: Energy Access Diagnostic Report Based on the Multi-Tier Framework," June 2018, https://openknowledge.worldbank.org/bitstream/handle/10986/30101/129101-ESM-P156666-PUBLIC-MTF-Energy-Access-Country-Diagnostic-Report-Rwanda-6-2018.pdf?sequence=1&isAllowed=y

[32] World Bank, "Rwanda Systematic Country Diagnostic," June 25, 2019, http://documents.worldbank.org/curated/en/219651563298568286/pdf/Rwanda-Systematic-Country-Diagnostic.pdf

[33] World Bank, "Report No.24503-Rw, the Republic of Rwanda Poverty Reduction Strategy Paper, Joint IDA-IMF Staff Assessment", July 18, 2002, (Retrieved September 14, 2019, http://documents.worldbank.org/curated/en/345831468759882378/pdf/multi0page.pdf

[34] World Bank, "Poverty headcount ratio at $1.90 a day (% of population)," https://data.worldbank.org/indicator/SI.POV.DDAY?most_recent_value_desc=true

families whose main source of income is agriculture"[35] and that poverty reduction "was almost stagnant between 2014 and 2017."[36]

Alongside this dismal social and economic record was an even more depressing practice of human rights that included the following, according to the US Department of Justice's *Rwanda 2018 Human Rights Report*:

> "Unlawful or arbitrary killings by state security forces; forced disappearance by state security forces; torture by state security forces including asphyxiation, electric shocks, mock executions; arbitrary detention by state security forces; political prisoners; arbitrary or unlawful interference with privacy; threats to and violence against journalists, censorship, website blocking, and criminal libel; substantial interference with the rights of peaceful assembly and freedom of association … and restrictions on political participation."[37]

And then, Kagame gave himself immunity for life with a constitutional amendment that reads, "A former President of the Republic cannot be prosecuted for treason or serious and deliberate violation of the Constitution when no legal proceedings in respect of that offence were brought against him or her while in office."[38]

---

[35] World Bank, "Agricultural Development in Rwanda", January 23, 2013, retrieved September 15, 2019, https://projects-beta.worldbank.org/en/results/2013/01/23/agricultural-development-in-rwanda

[36] World Bank, "Rwanda Systematic Country Diagnostic," June 25, 2019, https://openknowledge.worldbank.org/bitstream/handle/10986/32113/Rwanda-Systematic-Country-Diagnostic.pdf?sequence=1&isAllowed=y

[37] US Department of Justice, "Rwanda 2018 Human Rights Report," Retrieved August 24, 2019, https://www.justice.gov/eoir/page/file/1146601/download

[38] Republic of Rwanda, The Constitution of The Republic of Rwanda Of 2003 Revised in 2015," Official Gazette Special of 24/12/2015, http://www.mininfra.gov.rw/fileadmin/user_upload/aircraft/RWANDA_CONSTITUTION_NEW_2015_Official_Gazette_no_Special_of_24.12.2015.pdf

The failure of Kagame's Faustian bargain—trading human rights for development and ending up with neither—should come as no surprise to students of history and human nature. An authoritarian who can't be questioned, an elite that dominates both the state and the economy, and an atmosphere of anxiety: these do not constitute the formula for social and economic development. In Rwanda, as elsewhere, people do their best work in an environment of freedom, not fear.

The dismal developmental outcomes and Kagame's violence raise an important question. How do we explain the persistence of men such as Clinton, Blair, and Kim in supporting Kagame despite the failure of his Faustian bargain? The most persuasive explanation comes from an unrelated work by an American historian, Stacy Cordery, a scholar of presidential families in the United States. According to Cordery, when most presidents retire, they cannot "resist the urge to stay relevant." She adds:

> "Some former presidents turn into elder statesmen, dispensing advice to all who will listen … Others have tarnished their reputations with exorbitant speaking fees or by vilifying their successors … In the end, the desire to reward and punish, to analyze the past, to promote an agenda, to be part of the nation's business, and to remain in the spotlight proves overwhelming … Ambitious men accustomed to prominence and power find it difficult to "retire from active life to rest."[39]

Clinton and Blair belong to that category of former elected politicians who seek to remain relevant while making serious money. American and British press regularly report how many millions the two men have made from speaking—mostly about fighting poverty. The

---

[39] Stacy A. Cordery, "In retirement, most ex-presidents can't resist the urge to stay relevant", The Conversation, June 20, 2018, https://theconversation.com/in-retirement-most-ex-presidents-cant-resist-the-urge-to-stay-relevant-97995

articles "And for My Second Act, I'll Make Some Money"[40] and "Tony Blair Has Used His Connections to Change the World, and to Get Rich"[41] from the *New York Times*, the CNN report "$153 million in Bill and Hillary Clinton Speaking Fees, Documented,"[42] and the *Guardian* article "The Former British PM Is Trousering Millions of Pounds from the International Lecture Circuit"[43] are examples of this reporting. To make speeches, Bill Clinton and Tony Blair need poor countries like Rwanda, which allow them to set up foundations seen as eradicating hunger, building better health systems, or reinforcing policymaking capacities of weak governments. Clinton and Blair need Kagame, just as Kagame needs them. They are in mutually beneficial relationships.

Jim Yong Kim's entry into Kagame's camp was Partners In Health, an international health charity that he cofounded that calls Rwanda "a global health model," in which "vaccination rates for many diseases surpass those reported in the United States."[44] Partners In Health has collaborated with the Clinton Health Access Initiative since the early 2000s, landing a scandalous US$150 million project in Rwanda in 2012, more about that later. Jim Yong Kim at the time was president of Dartmouth College, which was a participant in the US$150 million scandal. Predictably, Bill Clinton, Paul Farmer and Kagame successfully

---

[40] Katharine Q. Seelye, "And for My Second Act, I'll Make Some Money", September 9, 2007, *The New York Times*, https://www.nytimes.com/2007/09/09/weekinreview/09seelye.html

[41] Danny Hakim, The New York Times, "Tony Blair Has Used His Connections to Change the World, and to Get Rich," August 5, 2014, https://www.nytimes.com/2014/08/06/business/international/tony-blair-has-used-his-connections-to-change-the-world-and-to-get-rich.html

[42] Robert Yoon, "$153 million in Bill and Hillary Clinton speaking fees, documented", February 6, 2016, *CNN*, https://www.cnn.com/2016/02/05/politics/hillary-clinton-bill-clinton-paid-speeches/index.html

[43] The Guardian, "The former British PM is trousering millions of pounds from the international lecture circuit", April 10, 2009, https://www.theguardian.com/politics/blog/2009/apr/10/tony-blair-speaking-fees

[44] Partners In Health, "How Rwanda Went from Genocide to Global Health Model," https://www.pih.org/media-coverage/global-post-how-rwanda-went-from-genocide-to-global-health-model

campaigned for Kim to head the World Bank. In other words, Kim was a Kagame enthusiast long before he became the president of the World Bank.

Once again, it was Kagame's manipulative skill that equipped him to independently grasp historian Cordery's insight that former high-office holders need global limelight and money—a need that Kagame cunningly exploited. Beyond their rhetoric, however, Kagame's donors and supporters realize that Vision 2020 was a fiasco. That is why they invented the contradictory term "an impressive economic performer but poor country" to describe Rwanda. To its credit, the IMF has been more cautious in its views on Rwanda. As the IMF explains, "despite the notable achievements, external risks could pose hurdles to Rwanda's quest towards achieving middle-income status," rightly noting that "the structural reform agenda should continue encouraging more private investment." Unlike the praise-singing World Bank, the IMF is also aware of perennial risks that include "regional political issues." The IMF concludes that the available resources in Rwanda currently "fall far short of what will be needed to realize the longer-term development objectives."[45]

Kagame, however, remains unwavering in claiming that he built a middle-income economy. When asked on November 8, 2019, to assess the success rate in the implementation of Rwanda Vision 2020, Kagame declared his performance outstanding. As he put it, "we will have achieved 85 percent of the targets by 2020."[46] Completion of a national development plan cycle of this magnitude would ordinarily call for a comprehensive evaluation. Such a stock-taking exercise would establish the lessons learned for improving successor visioning, strategy and planning. National stakeholders and sector specialists would indicate what worked and what did not. This is not the Kagame way. He did not

---

[45] International Monetary Fund, "Rwanda: Tenth Review Under the Policy Support Instrument", November 2018, file:///C:/Users/David/Downloads/cr18335%20(1).pdf
[46] President Paul Kagame, "Press Conference with President Kagame," Kigali, 8 November 2019 https://youtu.be/IVr_csxBbME

conduct any kind of evaluation at the end of the twenty-year period of Rwanda Vision 2020. Kagame instead boasted on December 19, 2019 as follows:

> "When we embarked on Vision 2020, Rwanda had no airline to speak of. Now RwandAir reaches 28 destinations, with more planned. The new airport will take our aviation sector to the next level…We are now able to finance 84 per cent of our national budget… We might achieve 8.5% growth by the end of this year. That's an unequalled record…Our economy has maintained a high growth rate every year, accompanied by reductions in poverty. This year, our economy grew even more than usual…Last year, I had predicted that 2019 would be better than 2018; we can see now that it was true. Now I can predict that 2020 will also be better than 2019."[47]

Self-aggrandizement and preordained answers sufficed for Kagame, namely that Rwanda is already an African economic lion growing at unequalled record. That is how the Rwandan ruler sustains his Faustian bargain. To justify the human rights tradeoff, Kagame must claim spectacular social and economic success.

---

[47] Paul Kagame, State of The Nation Address 17th Umushyikirano, December 19, 2019, https://twitter.com/UrugwiroVillage/status/1207626776253550592

CHAPTER 2

Kagame's Relentless Global Marketing of Middle-Income Economy Mirage

Long before 2020, the year when Rwanda was to reach its milestone of becoming a middle-income economy, Kagame had declared, "Mission accomplished." After declaring in 2013 that Rwanda was an economic lion, Kagame announced in 2016 that Rwanda had now completed building economic infrastructure and the institutional foundation to the extent that a timetable for ending foreign aid must be set. Rwanda was on its way to self-reliance and ready to end the stigma of depending on foreign aid handouts, said Kagame. In his state of the nation address in 2016 Kagame stated:

> "We stand at a moment of transition. So, it is a good moment to take stock of the various stages of our journey together thus far and look toward the road ahead. The first phase, starting 22 years ago, was about security and national unity. A sense of safety and belonging was restored. ... That brings us to the most recent period where we have been building the infrastructure needed to connect us to the global economy, while also getting Rwandans ready to work smartly in a more competitive environment. ... Rwanda is the second easiest place in Africa to do business, according to the World Bank.

We used to struggle just to survive. Now we struggle
to thrive and prosper. ... The main barrier we face is
internal. ... An example is something we have been
talking about for a long time, the issue of relying on
others to pay for things that benefit us. It is really a
question of dignity, our *agaciro*. Therefore, among the
decisions of this *Umushyikirano*, we should resolve to set
a deadline, which should come sooner rather than later,
after which Rwanda will no longer be waiting for what
others hand out to us."[48]

To spread this narrative and champion his qualities as a visionary
leader transforming Rwanda into a middle-income economy, Kagame
used five strategies. First, he mobilized an extraordinarily influential
group of personalities in the global power centers of Washington,
London, and Brussels. Kagame courted people like former US president
Bill Clinton and his wife, Hillary Clinton; former British prime minister
Tony Blair and his wife, Cherie Blair; another former UK prime minister
David Cameron, Susan Rice, who was Bill Clinton's assistant secretary
of state for Africa, later becoming President Barack Obama's national
security adviser after serving as US ambassador at the UN; British
minister for international development Andrew Mitchell, World Bank
president Jim Yong Kim, and the European Union's commissioner for
development aid Louis Michel. Below the top elite group were other
prominent personalities, which included Michael Porter of Harvard
University's Business School; Sir David King, the chief scientific
adviser to the UK government under both Tony Blair and Gordon
Brown; the American preacher Rick Warren; Sir Thomas Hunter, a
Scottish billionaire businessman; and Howard Buffett—eldest son of
multibillionaire investor Warren Buffett.

The second strategy used by this astounding schemer was to hire
public relations firms to popularize him in the West. For example, for

---

[48] Paul Kagame, "State of The Nation Address 14th Umushyikirano", December 15,
2016, retrieved September 8, 2019, http://paulkagame.com/?p=5188

a monthly fee of US$50,000 and up to US$3,500 for monthly out of pocket costs to cover travel, the Boston-based W2 Group promoted "President Kagame and his visionary leadership, including his adoption of democratic principle and free markets as a means of elevating Rwanda." The Kagame promotional campaign targeted, among others,

> "global political elites in key government centers, specifically Washington, D.C. and Brussels. ... Elites in both capitals will include: a) Elected officials (particularly those serving on committees with direct impact on African and Rwandan policy decisions); b) Aids and staffers to these elected officials; c) NGOs, GSAs and aid organizations that work within the African and Rwandan community. ... Concurrently, we will focus on Rwanda's business advancement narrative ... in places like *The Financial Times*, *The Wall Street Journal*, *Forbes* and *Fortune*. ... We will proceed with a series of visits by top tier names in government, post-genocidal recovery, economic development and other key areas to Rwanda. While visiting, we may want to schedule television and radio broadcast dialogues, joint interviews with President Kagame and other events and appearances that can be merchandised via global media. ... We will secure speaking engagements for President Kagame and other top Rwandan government and private sector officials as top tier political science and business colleges throughout the US, Europe and Asia."[49]

In the third strategy, Kagame actively sought and found jobs for his cabinet ministers and senior public servants in influential international organizations whose decisions impacted Rwanda. Kagame heavily

---

[49] US Department of Justice, Foreign Agents Registration by W2 Group Inc on "Master Service Agreement by and between Government of Rwanda and W2 Group, Inc.", August 12, 2011, https://efile.fara.gov/docs/6055-Exhibit-AB-20110812-1.pdf

campaigned for his minister of finance, Donald Kaberuka, to become the president of the African Development Bank (AfDB), the continent's principal financing agency. With donors votes in AfDB, Kagame and Kaberuka won. The governor of Rwanda National Bank, Laurean Rutayisire, and senior economist in the office of the president, Gaston Mpatswe, were posted to the International Monetary Fund (IMF). The deputy governor of the National Bank of Rwanda, Consolata Rusagara, was transplanted into the World Bank and is practice manager in the Finance, Competitiveness, and Innovation Global Practice. Former minister in the office of the president, Patrick Mazimhaka was posted to the African Union as Deputy Chairperson of the African Union Commission. Kagame's minister of education, Romain Murenzi, was made the executive director of the World Academy of Sciences. Kigali mayor Aisa Kirabo Kacyira became the assistant secretary-general and deputy executive director for UN-HABITAT. Agnes Binangwaho, who was Kagame's health minister and family doctor, became vice-chancellor of the University of Global Health Equity, established by Partners In Health, the brainchild of Paul Farmer and Jim Yong Kim. Former Kagame's agriculture minister, Agnes Kalibata, is the president of the Alliance for a Green Revolution in Africa. Louise Mushikiwabo, Kagame's foreign minister, was appointed to the position of secretary-general of the Organisation Internationale de la Francophonie. Richard Sezibera was posted into the East African Community Secretariat as its secretary-general before returning to Rwanda to become Kagame's foreign minister.

Kagame's fourth self-marketing strategy revolved around the man himself. He became his own salesman, traveling year-round in different parts of the world, selling his brand of a visionary leader and African statesman. Kagame barely stays in Rwanda—it is most unlikely that another head of state travels outside his country like Kagame does. Between January and December 2019, for example, Kagame attended fifty-nine overseas events:

1. Attending the Doha Forum | Doha, Qatar, 14 December 2019.

2. Attending the 9th Summit of the ACP Heads of States and Governments| Nairobi, Kenya, 9 December 2019.

3. Attending the G20 Compact with Africa Investment Summit | Berlin, Germany, 19 November 2019.

4. Attending Africa Investment Forum | Johannesburg, South Africa, 11 November 2019.

5. Attending Russia-Africa Summit | Sochi, Russia, 23-24 October 2019.

6. State Visit to Central African Republic | Bangui, Central African Republic, 15 October 2019.

7. Attending the 8th CGECI Academy (Confédération Générale des Entreprises de Côte d'Ivoire) | Abidjan, Cote d'Ivoire, 14 October 20019.

8. Attending World Policy Conference 2019 | Marrakesh, Morocco, 12 October 2019.

9. Attending Rwanda Day Germany | Bonn, Germany, 5 October 2019.

10. Visiting the Bill and Melinda Gates Foundation | Seattle, USA, 2 October 2019.

11. Participating in World Leaders Forum - Columbia University | New York, USA, 26 September 2019.

12. Delivering statement at the 74th United Nations General Assembly - General Debate | New York, USA, 24 September 2019.

13. Holding Presidential Advisory Council Meeting | New York, USA, 22 September 2019.

14. Visiting Kenya | Nairobi, 18 September 2019.

15. Attending Tokyo International Conference on African Development | Yokohama, Japan, 27 August 2019.

16. Attending G7 Meeting | Biarritz, France, 24 August 2019.

17. Attending Quadripartite Summit | Luanda, Angola, 21 August 2019.

18. Making a state visit to Namibia |Windhoek, 20 August 2019.

19. Attending launch of SDGs Sub-Regional Centre for Southern Africa | Lusaka, 7 August 2019.

20. Witnessing signing of Peace and Reconciliation Agreement | Maputo, Mozambique, 6 August 2019.
21. Meeting with the Prince of Wales at Highgrove House in Gloucestershire, UK | July 23, 2019.
22. Attending Quadripartite Summit | Luanda, Angola, 12 July 2019.
23. Attending Extraordinary African Union Summit | Niamey, Niger, 7 July 2019.
24. Making state visit to Botswana | Gaborone, 28 June 2019.
25. Attending Madagascar on the 59th Anniversary of Independence, 27 June 2019.
26. Attending European Development Days. | Brussels, Belgium, 19 June 2019.
27. Attending national Democracy Day| Abuja, Nigeria, 12 June 2019.
28. Attending Anti-Corruption Summit | Abuja, Nigeria, 11 June 2019.
29. Visiting Gabon | Gabon, 10 June 2019.
30. Attending his son's graduation at Williams College | Williamstown, USA, June 2, 2019.
31. Visiting the Democratic Republic of Congo | Kinshasa, 31 May 2019.
32. Attending President Cyril Ramaphosa's inauguration, Pretoria, South Africa, 25 May 2019.
33. Attending his daughter's graduation at Columbia University | New York, USA, 19 May 2019.
34. Meeting with Young Presidents' Organization Paris Chapter | Paris, France, 17 May 2019.
35. Attending VivaTech2019 | Paris, France, 17 May 2019.
36. Attending 22nd Milken Institute Global Conference | Los Angeles, USA, 30 April 2019.
37. Attending World Economic Forum Center for 4th Industrial Revolution Business Roundtable | San Francisco, USA, 29 April 2019.

38. Attending Broadband Commission meeting for Sustainable Development | San Francisco, USA, 29 April 2019.

39. Watching Basketball |Oakland, USA, 29 April 2019.

40. Visiting Tarana Wireless Offices | San Francisco, USA, 28 April 2019.

41. Attending AU Troika Summit on Libya and Sudan | Cairo, Egypt, 23 April 2019.

42. Visiting Saddleback Church | California, USA, 14 April 2019.

43. Attending UN reflection on the 1994 Genocide in Rwanda |United Nations Headquarters | New York, USA, 12 April 2019.

44. Attending NBA Board of Governors Dinner | New York, USA, 11 April 2019.

45. Attending swearing-in of President Macky Sall of Senegal | Dakar, Senegal, 2 April 2019.

46. Working Visit to Angola | Luanda, Angola, 21 March 2019.

47. Working visit to Tanzania | Dar es Salaam, Tanzania, 8 March 2019.

48. Attending Young Presidents' Organization | Cape Town, South Africa, 5—6 March 2019.

49. Attending Fespaco 2019 | Ouagadougou, Burkina Faso, 2 March 2019.

50. Meeting with Business Leaders hosted by Hiinga | Charlotte USA, 18 February 2019.

51. Attending All-Stars Basketball | Charlotte USA, 17—18 February 2019.

52. Attending Munich Security Conference | Munich, Germany, 14 February 2019.

53. Attending Milken Middle East and North Africa Summit | Abu Dhabi, UAE, 13 February 2019.

54. Attending World Government Summit | Dubai, UAE, 13 February 2019.

55. Attending Ordinary Session of the African Union | Addis Ababa, Ethiopia, 11 February 2019.

56. Attending the 20th Ordinary Summit of the East African Community Heads of State | Arusha, Tanzania, 1 February 2019.
57. Attending the World Economic Forum | Davos, Switzerland, 22–24 January 2019.
58. Attending high-level consultation meeting of heads of state on the situation in DRC | Addis Ababa, Ethiopia, 17 January 2019.
59. Making an official visit to Japan | Tokyo, Japan, 8 January 2019.

Kagame's fifth self-promotion strategy is manipulating statistics to portray Rwanda as an African success story. A good example is the Rwanda Development Board's statistics. This is how RDB reported foreign investment in Rwanda for 2018:

"In the last 8 years, registered investments in Rwanda jumped from US$398 million in 2010 to slightly over US$2 billion in 2018. Last year, we passed the US$2 billion milestone, for the first time in the country's history. This is evidence that Rwanda is being seen increasingly as a great place to do business, innovate and establish a hub from which to access the continent's tremendous opportunities. The increased investments registered are a direct result of the initiatives that the Government of Rwanda, through RDB, has put in place to continuously make Rwanda an attractive destination for investment. In fact, this year, Rwanda was proudly ranked the 29th easiest place to do business in the world and the 2nd easiest place to do business in Africa."[50]

RDB's claims here are deceitful. Foreign direct investment (FDI) in Rwanda amounted to US$305 million in 2018, compared to Kenya at US$1.6 billion, Uganda at US$1.3 billion, and Tanzania at US$1.1

---

[50] Rwanda Development Board, "Rwanda Development Board registers over US$ 2 billion worth of investments in 2018," retrieved December 6, 2019, https://rdb.rw/rwanda-development-board-registers-over-us-2-billion-worth-of-investments-in-2018/

billion.[51] Meanwhile, cumulative foreign direct investment stock in Rwanda rose from US$55 million in 2000 to US$2.2 billion in 2018. Cumulative foreign direct investment stock in Kenya rose from US$932 million in 2000 to US$14 billion in 2018. Cumulative foreign direct investment stock in Uganda rose from US$807 million in 2000 to US$13 billion in 2018. In Tanzania, cumulative foreign direct investment stock rose from US$2.7 billion in 2000 to US$20 billion in 2018.[52] In other words, even though Rwanda is ranked by the World Bank as the 2nd easiest place to do business in Africa, it draws the least amount of FDI among its East African peers.

The Rwandan head of state's relentless marketing of delusional grandeur paid off. Clinton was among the early believers in Rwanda Vision 2020. Clinton congratulated Kagame for executing Rwanda development strategy "with discipline and passion, and as far as I can tell, unequalled anywhere else in the world. That is an enormous credit to the leadership of Paul Kagame."[53] For Clinton, Kagame's human rights tradeoff for economic development was worth it, as Clinton explained when confronted with Kagame's violence in DR Congo:

> "Its complicated by the fact that the section of Congo near Rwanda is full of people who perpetrated the genocide, who spurned the president's offer to come home and not go to prison and you can't get around the fact that the economic and social gains in Rwanda have

---

[51] World Bank, "Foreign direct investment net inflows," 2018, https://data.worldbank.org/indicator/BX.KLT.DINV.CD.WD

[52] United Nations Conference on Trade and Development, "World Investment Report," 2018, https://unctad.org/en/PublicationsLibrary/wir2019_en.pdf

[53] See "President Clinton speaks on achievements of Rwanda across all sectors and commits to assisting Rwanda's health sector in becoming free from foreign aid through partnership between the Ministry of Health, Clinton Initiative and 13 top US schools," published on July 20, 2012, https://www.youtube.com/watch?v=oUZWeBjjGc4&feature=youtu.be&list=PLEVvC9V_8948N YHq7PS4IeHSLZBOWhgC

been nothing short of astonishing under Kagame, and he says he's going to leave when his time's up."[54]

Britain's Blair agrees, stating that it is through Kagame's "visionary leadership that Rwanda has become the African success story it is today, a country moving in the right direction at a remarkable pace."[55] When challenged to account for supporting a human rights abuser, Blair's views mirror those of Clinton:

> "I'm a believer in and a supporter of Paul Kagame. I don't ignore all those criticisms, having said that. But I do think you've got to recognize that Rwanda is an immensely special case because of the genocide. Secondly, you can't argue with the fact that Rwanda has gone on a remarkable path of development."[56]

For the former British prime minister David Cameron, "Rwanda has been, and continues to be, a success story" and adds that he is "proud of the fact that the last Government, and this Government, have continued to invest in that success. ... I continue to believe that investing in Rwanda's success, as one of those countries in Africa that is showing that the cycle of poverty can be broken."[57] The World Bank talks of "Rwanda's visionary leadership and the institutions established

---

[54] Bill Clinton, "20 minutes with Bill Clinton - up against 'big poppa'", BBC Interview, August 12, 2013, https://www.bbc.com/news/world-africa-23632845

[55] See "Tony Blair hailed President Kagame's visionary leadership as he saw for himself the remarkable pace of Rwandan progress during a two-day visit to the East African country," November 16, 2009, https://institute.global/news/governance/praise-paul-kagame-during-latest-visit-rwanda

[56] Chris McGreal, "Tony Blair defends support for Rwandan leader Paul Kagame," The Guardian, December 31, 2010, https://www.theguardian.com/world/2010/dec/31/tony-blair-rwanda-paul-kagame

[57] David Cameron, Engagements Oral Answers to Questions, Prime Minister in the House of Commons at 11:30 am on 17th October 2012, https://www.theyworkforyou.com/debates/?id=2012-10-17c.317.1

during the nation-building of the 1990s and early 2000s."[58] Addressing the question of electricity in Rwanda, former World Bank Robert Zeolleck stated that "Rwanda has the capacity to be a leader for the rest of Africa, showing that these policies can be implemented and showing how it will be done."[59] Former World Bank president Jim Yong Kim asserts tha*t* "Rwanda has always been looking three steps, four steps ahead of anyone else" and that "Rwanda has managed its economy brilliantly." Kim further states that it was "a tremendous privilege to be witnessing the tremendous growth and innovation happening in Rwanda."[60] Louis Michel, former European commissioner for development and humanitarian aid, asserts that "few countries have had as much success in delivering the MDGs than Rwanda" and that Rwanda is an "inspiration to the international community as they decide the sustainable economic, social and environment goals which will drive our collective efforts to build a fairer and prosperous world."[61] For Howard Buffett, Kagame must remain in power or investors will not put their money in Rwanda. "Investors want stability and Rwanda is exactly that. If we didn't think President Kagame was going to be here for another 7 years we wouldn't even, consider being here."[62]

More recently, the World Bank declared Rwanda a global star in 2019. According to the World Bank, Rwanda had by 2019 surpassed Japan,

---

[58] World Bank, "Rwanda Systematic Country Diagnostic", June 25, 2019 http://documents.worldbank.org/curated/en/219651563298568286/pdf/Rwanda-Systematic-Country-Diagnostic.pdf

[59] Robert Zoellick, "World Bank President Praises Rwanda's Energy Sector," August 12, 2009, http://web.worldbank.org/WBSITE/EXTERNAL/NEWS/0,,contentMDK:22275423~pagePK:34370~piPK:34424~theSitePK:4607,00.html

[60] Jim Yong Kim's remarks, "President Kagame receives World Bank Group President," March 22, 2017, http://paulkagame.com/?p=5357

[61] Louis Michel, "Rwanda's track record on MDGs should inspire others", EURACTIV.COM, Sept 26, 2013, https://www.euractiv.com/section/development-policy/opinion/rwanda-s-track-record-on-mdgs-should-inspire-others/

[62] Howard Buffett, Transcript, "President Kagame, Tony Blair, Howard Buffett speak at WEF," May 11, 2016, retrieved September 8, 2019, http://paulkagame.com/?p=4801

China, Switzerland, India, and other leading economies in creating one of the best business-friendly environments in the world. Rwanda moved eleven places to the twenty-ninth position out of 190 countries in the ease of doing business rankings.[63] The World Bank announced an even more spectacular achievement by Rwanda. "Rwanda continues to be the top performer,"[64] said the bank, in terms of economic management, policymaking, and institutional capabilities, areas in which "Rwanda continued to lead at the regional level and globally."[65] It was in this context that Rwanda and the World Bank crafted *"Future Drivers of Growth in Rwanda."*[66] Through this strategy, Rwanda will elevate itself from the lower-middle-income status of US$1,240 per capita, achieved in 2020, to become upper-middle-income status of US$4,035 per capita in 2035, reaching a high-income status of US$12,476 by 2050.[67]

What we see here is Kagame's audacity to sell hot air, side by side with the extraordinary willingness by prominent personalities in the West to buy hot air. Perhaps, the biggest delusion is Kagame's call for the timetable to end Rwanda's dependency on foreign aid. Official development assistance per capita in Rwanda is US$102, the second highest in East Africa after war-torn South Sudan. Foreign aid as percentage of Rwanda's central government expense is 70.9 percent,

---

[63] World Bank, Doing Business 2019," May 19, 2019, https://www.worldbank.org/content/dam/doingBusiness/media/Annual-Reports/English/DB2019-report_web-version.pdf

[64] World Bank, "Understanding the Africa country policy and institutional assessment (CPIA) 2017, September 12, 2018, https://www.worldbank.org/en/region/afr/publication/in-five-charts-understanding-the-africa-country-policy-and-institutional-assessment-cpia-report-for-2017,

[65] World Bank, "CPIA Africa: Assessing African Policies and Institutions," July 2018, http://documents.worldbank.org/curated/en/850151531856335222/pdf/128558-REVISED-WB-CPIA-Report-July2018-ENG-final-web.pdf

[66] World Bank, "Future Drivers of Growth in Rwanda," 2019, http://documents.worldbank.org/curated/en/522801541618364833/pdf/131875-V1-WP-PUBLIC-Disclosed-11-9-2018.pdf

[67] Claver Gatete, Minister of Finance, Republic of Rwanda, "Rwanda We Want: Towards Vision 2050," December 16, 2016, http://www.minecofin.gov.rw/fileadmin/user_upload/Hon_Gatete_Umushyikirano_Presentation_2016.pdf

while aid as a percentage of capital formation is 57.4 percent.[68] The high aid dependency is key evidence that Rwanda's economy has hardly changed structurally over the past two decades. Put in another way, Rwanda remains an exporter of raw materials, namely, tea, coffee, cassiterite, coltan, wolfram, hides and skin, pyrethrum, and re-exports— mainly to DR Congo, which earned Rwanda US$995 million in 2018. Meanwhile, Rwanda imports just about everything, including meat and fish, milk and milk products, eggs, natural honey, fats and oils of animal or plant origin, vegetables, fruit and spices, cereals, flours and seeds, various food preparations, salt and sugar, and sweets. In 2018, for example, out of Rwanda's import bill of US$2.2 billion, the imports of basic foodstuffs, at US$746 million, outstripped capital goods at US$620 million, intermediary goods at US$596 million, and energy and lubricants at US$252 million.[69] Rwanda's economy remains essentially informal, in which non-tradable goods and services produced and consumed domestically are predominant. As for the World Bank's enthusiasm for working with Rwanda to implement successor strategies to Vision 2020, this is a case of putting the cart before the horse. Before fantasizing about reaching upper-middle-income and high-income status, Rwanda needs first to emerge from the low-income category, where it remains stuck among the world's poorest economies.

---

[68] See World Bank data on "Net ODA received per capita (current US$)", "Net ODA received (% of central government expense)," and "Net ODA received (% of gross capital formation)," 2017, retrieved September 8, 2019, https://data.worldbank.org/indicator/DT.ODA.ODAT.CD

[69] For Rwandan imports, see National Bank of Rwanda, "Imports by Economic Destination 2018," file:///C:/Users/David/Downloads/FORMAL MONTHLY IMPORTS 2018.pdf. For Rwandan exports, see National Bank of Rwanda, "Monthly Exports 2018," file:///C:/Users/David/Downloads/FORMAL MONTHLY EXPORTS 2018%20(1).pdf

CHAPTER 3

Proof of Rwanda Vision 2020 Fiasco Comes from Rwanda Government and Its Diehard Supporter, the World Bank

The irony of ironies is that the Rwandan government's own statistics, and the data from its staunch supporter, the World Bank, demonstrate the failure of Vision 2020. Begin with the most basic life necessity, namely, food security. The 2018 comprehensive food security and vulnerability analysis conducted by the National Institute of Statistics of Rwanda, the Ministry of Agriculture and Animal Resources, and the World Food Programme paints a gloomy picture. Only 42.7 percent of Rwandan households are fully food secure, while 38.6 percent marginally food insecure and 18.7 are outright food insecure. In other words, besides the 18.7 percent of Rwandan households without access to enough quantity of affordable, nutritious food, 38.6 percent are on the borderline. These borderline households are precariously food secure as far as their current food consumption is concerned, but they do not have the ability to withstand the impact of climatic anomalies, such as drought and floods, which occur regularly in Rwanda. The food situation becomes clearer, however, when the Kigali Capital City's households, whose food insecurity is 2.2 percent, is removed from the equation. Then food insecurity rates skyrocket in rural Rwanda:

"The Western Province has the highest prevalence of food insecure households (29.9 percent), followed by the Southern Province (20.5 percent), Northern Province (17.8 percent) and Eastern Province (16.2 percent). … At district level, Rutsiro and Ngororero in the Western Province have the largest proportion of food insecure households (49.0 percent and 40.8 percent, respectively), followed by Kayonza (32.8 percent) in the Eastern Province, Nyamagabe (29.9 percent) in the Southern Province, Burera (29.7 percent) in the Northern Province, Nyabihu (25.7 percent) and Rusizi (25.3 percent) in the Western Province."[70]

Food insecurity, of course, comes from poverty. Put aside the fact that when we measure poverty in Rwanda using the US$3.20 a day, an indicator applied to middle-income economies, 80 percent of Rwandans are poor. Even at the international poverty line of US$1.90 a day applied to low-income economies, 55.5 percent or 6.6 million people out of Rwanda's 12 million population are poor. In comparative terms, Rwanda is the eleventh poorest country in the world, based on the international poverty line of US$1.90 a day, as indicated in Table 1.

Table 1. Rwanda poverty headcount in global perspective

Country	Percentage of population living on less than US$1.90 a day
1. Madagascar	77.6
2. DR Congo	76.6
3. Burundi	71.8
4. Malawi	70.3

[70] National Institute of Statistics of Rwanda, Ministry of Agriculture and Animal Resources, and World Food Programme, "Rwanda 2018 | Comprehensive food security and vulnerability analysis," December 2018, https://docs.wfp.org/api/documents/WFP-0000103863/download/

5. Guinea-Bissau	67.1
6. Central African Republic	66.3
7. Mozambique	62.4
8. Uzbekistan	62.1
9. Lesotho	59.7
10. Zambia	57.5
11. Rwanda	55.5

Source: World Bank Poverty Headcount Data

Table 2 indicates that Rwanda has the highest poverty headcount in the Eastern Africa region, except for Burundi, a country experiencing conflict. Ethiopia and Kenya have the lowest percentages of poverty at 27.3 percent and 36.8 percent, respectively. Tanzania, South Sudan, and Uganda follow in that order.

Table 2. Rwanda poverty headcount in regional perspective

Country	Percentage of population living on less than US$1.90 a day
1. Burundi	71.8
2. Rwanda	55.5
3. Tanzania	49.1
4. South Sudan	42.7
5. Uganda	41.7
6. Kenya	36.8
7. Ethiopia	27.3

Source: World Bank Poverty Headcount Data

Let us now look at Rwanda's specific sector circumstances, beginning with the foundations of human capital—namely, health and education. Table 3 highlights the health situation in Rwanda.

Table 3. Physician and pharmacist ratios to Rwandan population

Category	Status
1. Number of physicians in Rwanda	1,350
2. Physician per population in five urban districts of Gasabo, Kicukiro, Nyarugenge, Muhanga and Huye	1 doctor per 7,000 people
3. Physician per population in 7 districts of Karongi, Nyamasheke, Rusizi, Rubavu, Musanze, Rwamagana and Kayonza with mixed urban-rural population	1 per 7,000–15,000 people
4. Physician per population in rural districts of Nyaruguru, Nyamagabe, Nyanza, Kirehe, Gatsibo, Nyagatare Nyabihu and Rutsiro	1 doctor per 25,000–60,000 people
5. Number of pharmacists in Rwanda	87
6. Pharmacist per population	1 per 138,398

Source: Rwanda Ministry of Health, 2018

In contrast to the World Health Organization's recommendation of one physician per 1,000, Rwanda's ratios range from one doctor per 7,000 in urban areas to one doctor serving between 7,000 to 15,000 in semi-urban areas. In the case of rural districts, the ratios jump to one doctor serving between 25,000 to 60,000. The pharmacist to population ratio is an utter disaster—there is only one pharmacist per 138,398 people.[71]

Table 4. Key indicators in Rwanda's education sector

Category	Status (%)

---

[71] Republic of Rwanda, Ministry of Health, "Report of Development of Rwanda Master Facility List", Final Report, November 2018, http://www.moh.gov.rw/fileadmin/user_upload/policies/Validated%20Report%20of%20Rwanda%20Master%20Facility.pdf

1.	Net enrollment in pre-primary schools	20.8
2.	Net enrollment in primary schools	98.3
3.	Promotion rate in primary schools	80.0
4.	Net enrollment rate in secondary schools	30.4
5.	Percentage of trained staff in secondary schools	59.7
6.	Gross enrollment rate in tertiary institution	7.8

Source: Rwanda Ministry of Education, 2018

In the education sector, as indicated in table 4, even where Rwanda made progress at the primary school level with enrollment of 98.3 percent, serious challenges remain. For example, in Rwanda public schools, the average number of students in a classroom is eighty-five.[72] Furthermore, "the high rate of repetition is observed in primary 1 at the rate of 20.5% and in primary 5 at the rate of 14.0%. The high dropout rate is observed in primary 6 at 8.6% and primary 2 at 6.6%."[73] Secondary-school education is most worrying, however, as the Rwandan Ministry of Education indicates:

> "The Net Enrollment Rate (NER) at secondary level is still low because if only 30.4% of population aged between 13 and 18 are attending secondary schools it means that the remaining 70.2% of children who were expected to be in secondary school are not enrolled in this level. Some of them might still be in primary or out of the system. Causes of this case vary from district to district. A deep survey is to be conducted to tackle the cause and suggest solution."[74]

---

[72] Republic of Rwanda, Ministry of Education, "2018 Education Statistics," December 2018, http://197.243.16.104/~mineduc/newweb/fileadmin/user_upload/pdf_files/2018_Rwanda_Education_Statistics.pdf

[73] Ministry of Education, 2018 Education Statistics, Ibid.

[74] Ministry of Education, 2018 Education Statistics," Ibid.

And then, there is the gross enrollment in Rwanda's tertiary institutions, which stands at 7.8 percent.[75] Further, of those enrolled in tertiary institutions, "relatively few graduates are specializing in key job creation fields, such as science and engineering. Just 6 percent of university students in Rwanda are enrolled in engineering, manufacturing, and construction courses, and only 9 percent are studying sciences."[76]

The poor education outcomes spill into the Rwandan labor market comprising 7,130,333 working population aged sixteen and above, but of whom only 3,258,935 are in paid employment. The proportion of the Rwandan labor force that completed primary education or have no education is 78.4 percent, while 8.3 percent and 4.4 percent have lower secondary school and tertiary education, respectively. The largely low-skill workforce in Rwanda is not surprising because employment opportunities are essentially in low-skill sectors of agriculture, wholesale, retail, repair of motor vehicles and motorcycles as shown in Table 5. Tellingly, wages in Rwanda are dismal. The median monthly earnings in Rwanda is RWF20,800, or US$22 which becomes US$0.73 dollars a day.[77] In other words, the median daily earning of a Rwandan worker is less than a half of the international poverty line at US$1.90 a day.

Table 5. Key indicators in Rwanda's labor market and workforce

Category	Status
1. Rwanda population	12,374,397
2. Working-age population (16 years older and over)	7,130,333

---

[75] Ministry of Education, 2018 Education Statistics," Ibid.

[76] World Bank, "Rwanda: Systematic Diagnostic Report," June 2019, https://openknowledge.worldbank.org/bitstream/handle/10986/32113/Rwanda-Systematic-Country-Diagnostic.pdf?sequence=1&isAllowed=y

[77] Republic of Rwanda, National Institute of Statistics of Rwanda, "Labour Force Trends," Second Quarter," May 2019, file:///C:/Users/David/Downloads/Labour%20Force%20Survey%20Trend%20Report,%20May%20(Q2)%202019%20(1).pdf

3. Employed	3,258,935
4. Employed in agriculture	1,239,782
5. Employed in wholesale, retail trade, repair of motor vehicles and motorcycles	469,466
6. Employed in construction	295,800
7. Composite measure of labor underutilization (unemployed, underemployed, and potential labor force)	55%
8. Workforce that completed primary school or has no education	78.4%
9. Workforce that completed lower secondary school	8.3%
10. Workforce that completed tertiary education	4.4%
11. Median monthly earnings at main job	RWF20,800, or US$22.8
12. Percentage of large taxpayers	0.2
13. Percentage of medium taxpayers	0.5
14. Percentage of small and micro taxpayers	99.3
15. Number of listed companies on Rwanda Stock Exchange	8 of which 4 are Kenyan
16. Market capitalization in US$	3,199,895,469

Source: National Institute of Statistics of Rwanda, 2019; Rwanda Revenue Authority, 2018; Rwanda Stock Exchange, 2018.

The employer situation in Rwanda is much worse than that of workers. The number of taxpayers in Rwanda is 172,988, of whom "375 are categorized as large taxpayers (0.2%); 850 are medium taxpayers (0.5%) and 171,763 are small or micro taxpayers (99.3%)."[78] A small business in Rwanda is defined as a company with a tiny annual turnover

---

[78] Republic of Rwanda, Rwanda Revenue Authority, "Annual Activity Report 2017/18," October 2018, https://www.rra.gov.rw/fileadmin/user_upload/rra_annual_activity_report_2017-18.pdf

of less than RWF20,000,000, or US$21,900.[79] In other words, 99.3 percent of Rwandan companies have an annual turnover of US$21,900 or less. Meanwhile, there are eight companies listed on Rwanda Stock Exchange (RSE), of which four are Kenyan companies, while RSE market capitalization is a mere US$3.4 billion. RSE lists only one manufacturing company, Bralirwa Plc, part of Heineken Group, which makes beer, and the Coca-Cola bottler in Rwanda.[80]

As for infrastructure, the national utility company, Rwanda Energy Group, concedes that Rwanda's electricity sector is tiny, with installed 221.9 megawatts as opposed to available 154.1 megawatts. Rwanda's available electricity of 154 megawatts is equivalent to one Google solar farm in Alabama that produces 150 megawatts.[81] Further, in Rwanda, "the annual addition of the generating capacity required to expand the system is still very small."[82] The energy sector is so poorly run that the 2017 auditor-general's report concluded that "the delayed and abandoned contracts mainly comprised of energy and water projects" amounted to RWF206,817,279,066, or US$224.8 million, in 2017.[83] In the logistics sector, plans to connect Rwanda to the ports of Dar es Salaam, Tanzania or Mombasa in Kenya with a railway remain on the drawing board since the 2000s. It takes at least a week to transport Rwandan imports and exports to Mombasa and Dar Es Salaam, a

---

[79] Republic of Rwanda, "Law Nᵒ 016/2018 Of 13/04/2018 Establishing Taxes On Income," Official Gazette nᵒ16 of 16/04/2018, https://www.primature.gov.rw/index.php?id=2&no_cache=1&tx_drblob_pi1%5BdownloadUid%5D=464

[80] Rwanda Stock Exchange, "Monthly Statistics," June 2018, http://www.rse.rw/site/monthly_report

[81] Google, "Why we are putting 1.6 solar panels in Tennessee and Alabama," published in January 16, 2019, https://www.blog.google/outreach-initiatives/sustainability/why-were-putting-16-million-solar-panels-tennessee-and-alabama/

[82] REG, "Rwanda Least Cost Power Development Plan (LCPDP) 2019 – 2040," June 2019, http://www.reg.rw/fileadmin/user_upload/LCPDP_REPORT_June_2019.pdf

[83] Republic of Rwanda, Auditor General, "Report of The Auditor General of State Finances for The Year Ended 30 June 2017," http://www.oag.gov.rw/fileadmin/user_upload/Financial_Reports/ANNUAL_REPORT_JUNE_2017_EXECUTIVE_SUMMARY.pdf

journey that would be reduced to a day with a rail connection, thereby sharply reducing the cost of shipping. In 2018, the government described the situation as follows:

> "The Dar es Salaam-IsakaKigali/Keza-Musongati (DIKKM) Railway Project jointly implemented by the governments of Tanzania, Rwanda and Burundi is still underway. Feasibility studies and technical assistance sponsored by AfDB were completed in July 2014. … The construction of the Standard Gauge Railway (SGR) from Mombasa-Nairobi; Nairobi-Malaba; Malaba to Kampala and Kampala-Kigali, the Preliminary Engineering Design was completed and approved. Partner States are mobilizing funds for construction works."[84]

In February 2019, however, in a political conflict that remained unresolved up to the time of writing this book, Kagame closed the common border with Uganda through which Rwanda's imports and exports transit to Mombasa, Kenya. Rwandans were prevented from crossing the border into Uganda and, by extension, Kenya.[85]

The sanitation sector is also bad news, especially when we look at Rwanda's *Water and Sanitation Sector Strategic Plan 2013/14– 2017/18*, which aimed "to reach 100% coverage rate by 2017."[86] By 2016, very little, if any, coverage had been achieved. This was indicated by another national sanitation policy, which indicated that Rwanda

---

[84] Republic of Rwanda, Rwanda Transport Development Agency, "Annual Report Fiscal Year 2017/2018, https://www.rtda.gov.rw/fileadmin/templates/documents/ Annual_Report_2017_2018_FINAL.pdf

[85] See for example Catherine Byaruhanga, BBC Africa, "How the Rwanda-Uganda border crossing came to a halt," 9 March 2019, https://www.bbc.com/news/ world-africa-47495476

[86] Republic of Rwanda, Ministry of Infrastructure, "Water and Sanitation Sector Strategic Plan 2013/14 -2017/18", June 2013, http://www.mininfra.gov.rw/fileadmin/ user_upload/infos/Water_and_Sanitation_SSP_June_2013.pdf

had not yet invested in sanitation systems for densified urban areas, except a "few small sewerage systems in Kigali." Major hotels, hospitals, office buildings, and some industries "have installed their own (pre-) treatment systems," but on the whole, "Rwanda has not implemented systematically the integrated solid waste management approach," which means that "problems arise at all stages of waste collection and disposal."[87] The Kigali sanitation situation was described by the 2017 *Rwanda State of Environment and Outlook Report* in the following terms:

> "Kigali residents use improved pit latrines as the option for domestic sanitation. The more modern semi-centralized waste-water treatment options are limited to large institutions such as hotels and government offices and a few upmarket residential estates. ... The sewage sludge from households and semi-centralized septic tanks are evacuated and transported to holding tanks. ... there is a need to increase access to sanitation from the current 7 per cent use of flush toilets in Kigali. Currently there are only three sewerage systems serving about 700 households."[88]

The auditor-general described the sanitation infrastructure in Kigali as follows:

> "For more than 30 years, all the collected waste in Kigali was being dumped in an open dumpsite at Nyanza in Kigarama Sector, Kicukiro District. The site had started becoming a threat to the environment and public health and a decision was taken to relocate it from Nyanza in

---

[87] Republic of Rwanda, Ministry of Infrastructure, "National Sanitation Policy," December 2016, http://www.mininfra.gov.rw/fileadmin/user_upload/new_upload/NATIONAL_SANITATION_POLICY_DECEMBER_2016.pdf

[88] Republic of Rwanda, Rwanda Environment Management Authority, "State of Environment and Outlook Report 2017," file:///C:/Users/David/Downloads/RwandaSOER2017lowres2.pdf

December 2011. A temporary site at Nduba Landfill was selected to be developed and serve as a transitional landfill for the CoK while waiting for the completion of a modern landfill. However, the audit identified that Nduba Landfill has not been developed to address the environmental and public health threats that caused the re-location from Nyanza. … This sewage is deposited into pits dug at Nduba site without proper disposal system with a high likelihood of overflowing down from the hilltop (where the unsanitary landfill is located) into the valley if it rains heavily."[89]

By 2019, Rwanda as a whole and Kigali, a city of over a million and a half, did not yet have sanitation infrastructure, including centralized sewage system. The IMF observed in July 2019 that "only 13 percent of the population has access to safely managed sanitation (which includes containment through safe collection, treatment, and end use/disposal)."[90] On September 13, 2019, the Water and Sanitation Corporation declared that the waters of Nyabarongo, the 297 km river that supplies water to most parts of Rwanda, including Kigali, could not be "treated":

"Dear Customers; Nyabarongo water has become too turbid to be treated. This will affect water supply in the following areas: Nyarutarama, Kibagabaga, Bumbogo, Gihogere, Rukiri, Ruturusu, Nyagatovu, Nyabisindu and Bibare. Rwimbogo and Gasaraba will be affected too."[91]

---

[89] Republic of Rwanda, Auditor General, "Report of The Auditor General of State Finances for the Year Ended 30 June 2015," http://www.oag.gov.rw/fileadmin/user_upload/Procurement/Annual_Report_2015.pdf

[90] IMF, "Staff Report For The 2019 Article IV Consultation and Request for A Three-Year Policy Coordination Instrument," July 2019, https://www.imf.org/-/media/Files/Publications/CR/2019/1RWAEA2019001.ashx

[91] Republic of Rwanda, Water and Sanitation Corporation, "Nyabarongo water has become too turbid to be treated," September 13, 2019, retrieved September 15, 2019, https://twitter.com/wasac_rwanda/status/1172620637405364229?s=21

River Nyabarongo troubles, however, are largely due to the government's agricultural policies and unmanaged intensive cropland intensification that has over the years cleared a vast part of biomass cover by up to 76% of the land catchment. "Consequently, an estimated 409 million tons of soils are lost every year in the catchment and pollute the water of Nyabarongo River."[92]

The above government data and information line up with the World Bank's *Rwanda: Systematic Country Diagnostic Report*, and *Rwanda: Energy Access Diagnostic Report*, both published in June 2019. The two diagnostic reports are unusual documents for their candidness and because they depart from the World Bank's usual appeasement documents on Rwanda. Firstly, the energy diagnostic report categorically states that "Rwanda will not become a middle-income country by 2020 as Vision 2020 envisioned."[93] The *Rwanda: Systematic Country Diagnostic Report* analyses sector by sector, before advising how Rwanda needs to put its house in order if it is to pursue a genuine transformation agenda. *Rwanda Systematic Country Diagnostic Report* is summarized in table 6.[94]

---

[92] Fidele Karamage, Chi Zhang, Alphonse Kayiranga, Hua Shao, Xia Fang, Felix Ndayisaba, Lamek Nahayo, Christophe Mupenzi, and Guangjin Tian, "USLE-Based Assessment of Soil Erosion by Water in the Nyabarongo River Catchment, Rwanda", 20 August 2016, https://pdfs.semanticscholar.org/95eb/e6f1f95c59ea1d9029243dffe3bfc7f44c28.pdf

[93] World Bank, "Rwanda: Energy Access Diagnostic Report Based on the Multi-Tier Framework," June 25, 2019, http://documents.worldbank.org/curated/en/219651563298568286/pdf/Rwanda-Systematic-Country-Diagnostic.pdf

[94] World Bank, "Rwanda: Systematic Country Diagnostic Report," June 2019, http://documents.worldbank.org/curated/en/219651563298568286/pdf/Rwanda-Systematic-Country-Diagnostic.pdf

Table 6. Summary of the World Bank's *Rwanda Systematic Country Diagnostic Report*

Sector	Status
1. Poverty headcount	Poverty remains high at 55.5 percent, making Rwanda one of the poorest countries in the world.
2. Economy and exports	Rwanda exports less than low-income countries due to, among other things, a weak tradable sector.
3. Private sector	Despite Rwanda's *Doing Business* high ranking, the number of formal firms is about 10,000.
4. Foreign direct investment	Rwanda trails neighboring countries in attracting foreign direct investment.
5. Agriculture	Rwanda's agriculture is characterized by low productivity in absolute and relative terms compared to African countries.
6. Non-farm employment	Non-farm sectors are unable to create jobs and absorb labor from agriculture.
7. Large public investments and job creation	Conference infrastructure, which consumed US$1.5 billion in public investments, has not paid off.
8. Education	Rwanda trails low-income economies in education results.
9. Human capital	Rwanda's overall HCI is lower than the average low-income countries.
10. Economic Infrastructure	Half the rural population has no access to a road network in good condition within a 2 km walking distance.

11. Governance and institutions	Governance in Rwanda, a centralized, top-down decision-making approach, hampers innovation by local governments.
12. Corporate Governance	State enterprises, including Rwandan Patriotic Front companies, do not disclose ownership or annual financial results.
13. Foreign Aid	Foreign aid to Rwanda is nearly 5 percent more than the average for Africa and nearly double for low-income countries.

The data and analyses cited in this chapter come from the horse's mouth, so to speak—the materials are drawn from the main actor in the drama, namely, the government of Rwanda, and from the main supporting actor, the World Bank. It is important to note that the World Bank's *Rwanda: Systematic Country Diagnostic Report,* and *Rwanda: Energy Access Diagnostic Report*, were published in June 2019, five months after the departure of Jim Yong Kim from the bank. I am not privy to the inner workings of the World Bank, but these two documents repudiate the former World Bank president who had embarrassingly reduced himself to a Kagame propagandist. The publication of the two diagnostic reports was long over-due and a relief to researchers world-over who rightly regard the World Bank as a top-rate and objective knowledge institution as much as it is a development financier. We all depend on the World Bank for all manner of knowledge and information without which we would be poorer.

CHAPTER 4

CHAPTER 4

Confronted by the Vision 2020 Fiasco, Donors Retreated into Characterizing Rwanda an Impressive Economic Performer but Poor Country

Confronted with Rwanda Vision 2020 fiasco, donors changed the goalposts. They instead began to describe Rwanda in contradictory terms, namely that Rwanda is an impressive economic performer that remains one of the poorest in the world. Here are examples of how the donors use this irrational term of an impressive economic performer poor country, beginning with the IMF:

> "Rwanda has delivered impressive development outcomes in the past 20 years. ... Despite good progress to date, meeting the SDGs in a meaningful way will be challenging, with remaining gaps between NST goals and current basic service delivery. For instance, as of 2016, 38 percent of children still suffered from stunting and access to health facilities with qualified staff remained low ...; only 13 percent of the population has access to safely managed sanitation (which includes

containment through safe collection, treatment, and end use/disposal)."[95]

Here is the IMF again:

"Rwanda's high growth has raised income levels and reduced poverty, but incomes and labor skills are still catching up to peers. As a result of very rapid growth over the past 25 years, the per capita income has tripled. However, Rwanda's income levels remain below the average for Low-Income Countries (LICs)."[96]

Here is the World Bank's version of impressive economic performer but poor Rwanda:

"Rwanda is recognized as a leading reformer in Sub-Saharan Africa, with an impressive performance in poverty reduction. Annual gross domestic product (GDP) growth has averaged 7.5 percent in the last decade. ... Rwanda has also been the leading reformer among African economies in the Doing Business indicators: it moved from a global rank of 148 in 2008 to 29 in 2019, which is second in Africa after Mauritius. However, GDP per capita, which stood at US$787 in 2018, remains substantially below the average for Sub-Saharan Africa, and Rwanda remains one of the poorest countries in the world."[97]

Here is the World Bank again:

---

[95] IMF, "Staff Report for the 2019 Article IV Consultation and Request for A Three-Year Policy Coordination Instrument," Ibid.

[96] IMF, "Staff Report for the 2019 Article IV Consultation and Request for A Three-Year Policy Coordination Instrument," Ibid.

[97] World Bank, "Third Rwanda Energy Sector Development Policy Operation (P169040)," June 21, 2019," http://documents.worldbank.org/curated/en/361781562914743503/pdf/Appraisal-Program-Information-Document-PID-Third-Rwanda-Energy-Sector-Development-Policy-Operation-P169040.pdf

"In the past two decades, Rwanda has made impressive progress in terms of economic growth and reducing poverty. ... Despite these achievements in reducing poverty, Rwanda remains one of the poorest countries in the world. ... More than three out of four Rwandans, to a great extent located in rural areas, lack access to electricity. The electrification rate. ... remains largely concentrated in the top quintile, with almost negligible coverage in the bottom 40 percent of the population. ... Firms suffer from the high price of electricity compared to neighboring countries. Industries present electricity as a binding constraint, an important consideration as they are the ones most likely to drive job creation, exports, and growth."[98]

Here is the World Bank again with the concept of Rwanda as an impressive poor country:

"Rwanda has built a well-functioning system for basic education over the past 25 years, with impressive gains in widening access to primary education. The gross enrollment ratio (GER) in primary education rose from 123 percent in 2012 to 139 percent in 2017, putting Rwanda among Sub-Saharan African countries with the highest GERs. ... The survival rate in basic education is low, reflecting high dropout rates. ... In the World Bank's global assessment of learning for the human capital index, Rwanda scored 358 on a scale where 625 represents advanced attainment and 300 minimum

---

[98] World Bank, "Rwanda Energy Sector Development Policy Loan," March 20, 2017, http://documents.worldbank.org/curated/en/929971491367342885/pdf/AB7881-PGID-P162671-Concept-Stage-Box402900B-PUBLIC-Disclosed-4-4-2017.pdf

attainment. This puts Rwanda in the bottom quartile of countries assessed."[99]

Here is the World Bank yet again:

> "Rwanda's power sector has grown rapidly in the past decade and outpaced many of its peers in Sub-Saharan Africa. ... However, the cost of electricity supply is among the highest in the region. ... Household consumers have problems affording electricity at the present tariffs, a problem that will be aggravated as the rural electrification drive reaches ever poorer parts of the population. Especially larger firms report electricity as a binding constraint. ... The cost of electricity is among the 10 highest in SSA (around $0.25 per kilowatt hour in 2018). ... One-third (31.5 percent) of firms report that access to reliable electricity is a challenge to their operations. Power outages continue to cripple production and capacity utilization, as well as increases firms' costs due to low production or generator use."[100]

Here is the UK Department for International Development (DFID), asserting that "Rwanda has made more progress against the Human Development Index (an official indicator of life expectancy, education and income) than any other country in the world."[101] DFID adds, "Rwanda remains one of the poorest countries in the world. Over a third

---

[99] World Bank, "Project Appraisal Document on A Proposed Credit in the Amount Of SDR 145.2 Million (US$200.0 Million) To The Republic Of Rwanda for The Rwanda Quality Basic Education for Human Capital Development Project," July 9, 2019, http://documents.worldbank.org/curated/en/184411564797693303/pdf/Rwanda-Quality-Basic-Education-for-Human-Capital-Development-Project.pdf

[100] World Bank, "Lighting Rwanda: Rwanda Economic Update," June 2019, http://documents.worldbank.org/curated/en/593831561388957701/pdf/Rwanda-Economic-Update-Lighting-Rwanda.pdf

[101] DIFD, "Visit Rwanda's sponsorship of Arsenal FC," June 11, 2018, https://dfidnews.blog.gov.uk/2018/06/11/visit-rwandas-sponsorship-of-arsenal-fc/

of its population live in poverty."[102] DFID is not done. Rwanda has "a strong record of using aid effectively," but "poverty remains high."[103]

For the United States Agency for International Development, Rwanda "remains one of the world's poorest countries" but "the country's progress is remarkable."[104] Perhaps the strangest statement of an impressive economic performer but poor country comes from Kristalina Georgieva, the World Bank's chief executive officer. She places Rwanda among successful global players such as India and China but calls Rwanda a "tragedy" for its dismal human capital development:

> "Rwanda has climbed to a global rank of 29 compared to 41 last year. It is remarkable, because with seven reforms implemented in 12 months, the country is recognized as one of top 10 most-improved economies, alongside global players such as India and China. ... The World Bank's new Human Capital Index indicates that children born in Rwanda today will achieve just 37% of their potential. This is a tragedy."[105]

Georgieva misses the irony of her statement that a "remarkable" performer, recognized as one of the top-ten most-improved economies, is nonetheless a tragedy.

---

[102] Department for International Development (DIFD), "DIFID does not give any money to Rwandan sponsorship of Arsenal FC," May 27, 2018, https://dfidnews.blog.gov.uk/2018/05/27/mail-online-dfid-does-not-give-any-money-to-rwandan-sponsorship-of-arsenal-fc/

[103] DFID, "DFID Rwanda Profile, Planned Budget for 2018/2019 and 2019/2020," July 2018, https://assets.publishing.service.gov.uk/government/uploads/system/uploads/attachment_data/file/729951/DFID-Rwanda-Profile-July-2018.pdf

[104] USAID, "About Rwanda," Last updated: June 21, 2019, https://www.usaid.gov/rwanda

[105] Kristalina Georgieva, "Speech made after the launch of Rwanda's *The Future Drivers of Growth Report*," December 18, 2018, https://blogs.worldbank.org/nasikiliza/the-future-drivers-of-growth-in-rwanda

In one of his speeches, Kagame reminded his audience that he always chooses to think big. He added that "when we created Rwanda's Vision 2020 and committed to meeting our development goals—we were thinking big. When we decided to make Rwanda attractive for business—we were thinking big. When we invested in a broadband network that reaches all our 30 districts—we were thinking big."[106] It appears that foreign aid donors took Kagame's "thinking big" rhetoric on face value and fell into the same trap as he did—delusions of grandeur. The concept of an impressive economic performer but poor country is another delusion. No such country exists. Haiti, a country recognized as a failed state has a per capita income of US$868, which is higher than Rwanda's at US$773.[107] The failed state of Haiti outperforms the "impressive economic performer but poor state" of Rwanda. There is more bad news. In the 2019 World Bank study of fifteen countries that reduced extreme poverty by at least 1 percent annually between 2000 and 2015, of which seven are in Africa, Rwanda does not even feature. The seven African countries that reduced extreme poverty annually are Tanzania at -3.2 percent, Chad at -3.1 percent, Congo Republic at -2.7 percent, Burkina Faso at -2.4 percent, the Democratic Republic of Congo (DRC) at -2.3 percent, Ethiopia at -1.9 percent and Namibia at -1.6 percent.[108] DRC, a country often referred to as a failed state that keeps failing outperformed Kagame's African economic lion in annual extreme poverty reduction.

---

[106] Paul Kagame, "Speech by President Paul Kagame at the 20th Commemoration of the Genocide against the Tutsi," April 7, 2014, http://www.gov.rw/newsdetails2/?tx ttnews%5Btt news%5D=642&cHash=757dfe82a3bb4c2b1f9bbc2604186f81

[107] World Bank, "GDP per capita, current," 2018, https://data.worldbank.org/indicator/NY.GDP.PCAP.CD

[108] Miyoko Asai, Daniel Mahler, Silvia Malgioglio, Ambar Narayan, Minh Cong Nguyen, "Which Countries Reduced Poverty Rates the Most?", World Bank, November 12, 2019, https://blogs.worldbank.org/opendata/which-countries-reduced-poverty-rates-most.

CHAPTER 5

Kagame, the Clintons, Jim Yong Kim, and the Vulgarity of US Foreign Aid to Rwanda's Health Sector

While visiting his friend Kagame in 2012, Bill Clinton explained how he managed to convince the US Department of State to redirect money already programmed for fighting AIDS in Rwanda into his own health human resources development project in these terms:

> "What Clinton Health Access Initiative did was to approach a number of leading medical, nursing and health management schools … asking for a long-term commitment and a commitment at a lower cost. … To implement the plan, the government of Rwanda had to convince some of the largest donors, especially the United States to support the plan. They actually offered, the government of Rwanda did, to give up funding for existing programs so that the money can be redirected to develop the healthcare resources that your future requires. I have to say that I am very grateful to the US

government, to the Statement of State, which I happen
to think is well led."[109]

Clinton here is boasting of his wife's leadership in the State
Department—but more importantly, he is acknowledging his
unscrupulous lobbying of Hillary Clinton's State Department to divert
US$150 million from the AIDS program to his own health human
resources scheme in Rwanda.[110] As Annie Linskey put it, "State Dept.
aided Clinton-backed Rwanda effort: Bill Clinton wanted to build a
new health system in Rwanda. His wife's State Department delivered
big time."[111] Among the implementors of the Clinton scheme in Rwanda
was Farmer's and Jim Yong Kim's Partners In Health. Jim Yong Kim
himself was at the time the president of Dartmouth College, which,
predictably, joined the scheme, as the college later stated in a news
release:

> "Announced by Rwandan President Paul Kagame and
> former US President Bill Clinton in 2012, Rwanda's
> Human Resources for Health Program is a seven-year,
> $150 million collaboration between the US and Rwandan

---

[109] See "President Clinton speaks on achievements of Rwanda across all sectors
and commits to assisting Rwanda's health sector in becoming free from foreign
aid through partnership between the Ministry of Health, Clinton Initiative
and 13 top US schools," published on July 20, 2012, https://www.youtube.
com/watch?v=oUZWeBjjGc4&feature=youtu.be&list=PLEVvC9V_8948N
YHq7PS4IeHSLZBOWhgC

[110] Kevin Sack and Sheri Fink, "Rwanda Aid Shows Reach and Limits of Clinton
Foundation: In addition to doing good, the foundation enhances the Clinton brand,
never more than while Hillary Rodham Clinton is running for president," *The New
York Times*, October 18, 2015, https://www.nytimes.com/2015/10/19/us/politics/
rwanda-bill-hillary-clinton-foundation.html.

[111] Annie Linskey, "State Dept. aided Clinton-backed Rwanda effort: Bill Clinton
wanted to build a new health system in Rwanda. His wife's State Department
delivered big time," *Boston Globe*, October 17, 2015, https://www.bostonglobe.
com/news/politics/2015/10/17/state-department-under-hillary-clinton-redirected-
millions-for-bill-clinton-pet-project-rwanda/r7ASbc3E1HZ3JzriNRQAQI/story.
html

government and 25 leading US academic institutions, including the Geisel School of Medicine at Dartmouth, one of the founding partners. ... The program's $150 million budget is comprised of reallocated funding from the US President's Emergency Plan for AIDS Relief (PEPFAR) that is channeled directly to the Rwandan Ministry of Health. ... In an unprecedented move to improve efficiency of existing foreign aid, the US government redirected funds from projects completed by non-governmental organizations to the Ministry of Health, lowering administrative costs and freeing funds for the new program. ... The Clinton Health Access Initiative has helped to convene the American consortium of schools and academic medical centers. ... By the program's conclusion in 2018, Rwanda's specialist physician capacity will have more than tripled, and the proportion of the country's nurses with advanced training will have increased by more than 500%. ... Thereafter, the Rwandan government plans to fully finance the health workforce and medical education system on its own."[112]

As Clinton was launching his US$150 million scheme in Rwanda in 2012, he was also launching Kim's career at the World Bank. This is how Clinton championed Kim:

"Jim Kim is an inspired and outstanding choice to lead the World Bank based on his years of commitment and leadership to development and particularly health care and AIDS treatment across the world. Among his many accomplishments, his work with my good friend Paul

---

[112] Dartmouth College, "US Partners with Rwanda to Dramatically Expand Health Workforce Dartmouth Among Leading Medical Institutions Bridging Human Resource Gaps," November 20, 2013, https://geiselmed.dartmouth.edu/news/2013/11/20_rwanda/

Farmer to bring hope and health care to nations from Haiti to Peru to Malawi through Partners in Health has been pioneering, exceptional and effective. He will be the most experienced development expert to ever take the helm of the World Bank."[113]

Paul Farmer championed Kim in these terms:

"Jim Yong Kim is an outstanding choice for the presidency of the World Bank. Having had the good fortune to train with Jim at Harvard, and to see him work in settings from inner-city Boston to the slums of Peru, from Haiti to Rwanda to the prisons of Siberia, I know that for three decades Jim has committed himself to breaking the cycle of poverty and disease. This has been his goal as a physician, a teacher, a policy maker, and a university president; it was ever his goal as a founder and director of Partners In Health … I can think of no one more able to help families, communities, and entire nations break out of poverty, which is the stated goal of the World Bank. As poverty continues to claim lives, and as inequality deepens, the Bank—and other institutions charged with lessening poverty—need bold and experienced thinkers and implementers like Jim Kim. Alas, he's one of a kind."[114]

Kagame readily abandoned the candidate for the World Bank's presidency whom African nations supported in an effort to have more say in key international development agencies. African leaders had

---

[113] Bill Clinton recommendation of Jim Yong Kim, The White House, "Early Reactions to the Nomination of Jim Yong Kim as President of the World Bank," March 23, 2012, https://obamawhitehouse.archives.gov/the-press-office/2012/03/23/early-reactions-nomination-jim-yong-kim-president-world-bank

[114] Paul Farmer's recommendation of Jim Yong Kim, The White House, "Early Reactions to the Nomination of Jim Yong Kim as President of the World Bank," Ibid.

collectively nominated Ngozi Okonjo-Iweala, a seasoned professional who had spent a twenty-five-year career at the World Bank, rising to the number-two position of managing director, and was now Nigeria's finance minister. Kagame threw pan-Africanism and professionalism to the wind and stood by Jim Yong Kim and the Clinton camp instead. Kagame endorsed Kim as follows:

> "I was delighted to learn that Jim Kim has been nominated for this post, as he is a true friend of Africa and well known for his decade of work to support us in developing an efficient health system in Rwanda. He's not only a physician and a leader who knows what it takes to address poverty, but also a genuinely good person. President Obama's nomination of Dr. Kim as President of the World Bank is a welcome one and should resonate well with the many men and women who are working to transform lives around the world."[115]

Kagame rushed to meet Kim in Washington, "to discuss the importance of the World Bank's role in reducing poverty and supporting development for global economic growth" in a meeting that took place at the US Treasury Department on March 23, 2012.[116] And to whom did Jim Yong Kim turn for reforming the World Bank once he sat in the president's chair? Two men who are members of Kagame's Presidential Advisory Council, namely, Tony Blair[117] and Michael Porter.[118]

---

[115] Paul Kagame's recommendation of Jim Yong Kim, The White House, "Early Reactions to the Nomination of Jim Yong Kim as President of the World Bank," Ibid.

[116] US Treasury Department, "Dr Jim Kim meeting with Rwandan president Paul Kagame," March 23, 2012, https://www.flickr.com/photos/ustreasury/6877964630/

[117] World Bank, "Transcript: Delivering Results - A Conversation with Jim Yong Kim, Tony Blair, and Michael Barber," April 10, 2013," https://www.worldbank.org/en/news/speech/2013/04/10/delivering-results-conversation-jim-yong-kim-tony-blair-michael-barber

[118] Financial Times, "World Bank: Man on mission," April 7, 2014, https://www.ft.com/content/012f15d6-b8fa-11e3-98c5-00144feabdc0

Once in office, Kim would claim, for example, that "Rwanda has always been looking three steps, four steps ahead of anyone else" and that "Rwanda has managed its economy brilliantly." He would further declare that it was "a tremendous privilege to be here witnessing the tremendous growth and innovation happening here."[119] In 2018, Kim declared Kagame a global leader in human capital development. According to Kim, Kagame was committed to human capital to the extent that he was "rolling out mass media and radio campaigns to raise awareness and using conditional grants through its flagship social protection project to improve the delivery of health and nutrition services."[120] Here, Kim was attempting to turn Rwanda's disaster into a success story. In a report released four months earlier, the World Bank had sounded an alarm over chronic malnutrition in Rwanda, noting that "stunting rates are highest among the poorest households and those living in rural areas (nearly 50 percent), but even about 25 percent of children from the top two wealth quintiles suffer."[121] Clearly, Kim and Kagame had become co-propagandists working hard to mask the Rwanda Vision 2020 fiasco.

Before his resignation from the World Bank in February 1, 2019, it was announced that Kim would rejoin Partners In Health's board of directors. On January 7, 2019, Partners In Health announced, "Co-founder and World Bank Group President Dr. Jim Yong Kim will

---

[119] Jim Yong Kim's remarks, "President Kagame receives World Bank Group President," March 22, 2017, http://paulkagame.com/?p=5357

[120] Jim Yong Kim, "Remarks by World Bank Group President Jim Yong Kim at the 2018 Annual Meetings Plenary," October 12, 2018, HTTPS://WWW. WORLDBANK.ORG/EN/NEWS/SPEECH/2018/10/12/REMARKS-BY-WORLD-BANK-GROUP-PRESIDENT-JIM-YONG-KIM-AT-THE-2018-ANNUAL-MEETINGS-PLENARY

[121] World Bank, "Rwanda Economic Update: Tackling Stunting: An Unfinished Agenda," June 2018, http://documents.worldbank.org/curated/en/360651529100512847/pdf/127256-NWP-P164510-PUBLIC-Rwanda-Economic-Update-ed-no-12-June-2018.pdf

rejoin the global health non-profit's board of directors."[122] On August 12, 2019, Kim jetted to Rwanda to join the University of Global Health Equity (UGHE) commencement ceremony for the Masters of Science in Global Health Delivery.[123] The University of Global Health Equity was built in Rwanda by Partners In Health in the aftermath of the US$150 million scandal described earlier. The University of Global Health Equity describes the environment that created it while celebrating Kagame's visionary leadership and Rwanda as a spectacular global success story as follows:

> "By working closely with local governments and alongside communities to design and deliver public health programs, PIH has emerged as a leader in delivering health services in poor and under-resourced settings. Nowhere has this approach had more profound results than in Rwanda, which has achieved some of the most dramatic gains in population health and poverty reduction in the world...This visionary leadership, coupled with a commitment of infrastructure from the Government of Rwanda, have been invaluable to the success of UGHE, its graduates, and the communities in which they serve."[124]

Back in 2012, Clinton had boasted that over the course of the next seven years, "Rwanda will become a health education hub in Africa," predicting not only that Rwanda would train its health professionals, or just African health professionals, but that "people will come from all

---

[122] Partners In Health, "Partners In Health is pleased to announce that Partners In Health Co-founder and World Bank Group President Dr. Jim Yong Kim will rejoin the global health nonprofit's board of directors," January 7, 2019, https://www.pih.org/press/pih-welcomes-co-founder-dr-jim-yong-kim-back-board-directors

[123] New Times, "First Lady Jeanette Kagame joins UGHE commencement," August 12, 2019, https://www.newtimes.co.rw/news/first-lady-jeannette-kagame-joins-ughe-commencement-butaro

[124] University of Global Health Equity, "Our story," https://ughe.org/the-story-behind-the-university/

over the world to study this model." He further declared that within seven years, Rwanda would "be running a healthcare system without foreign assistance that will be the envy of Africa."[125] Did any of this materialize? In November 2018, Rwanda's health ministry described health professionals and population ratios as follows:

> "Five districts, namely Gasabo, Kicukiro, Nyarugenge, Muhanga and Huye, have already one doctor for less than 7,000 people. Other 7 districts (Karongi, Nyamasheke, Rusizi, Rubavu, Musanze, Rwamagana and Kayonza) have one doctor serving between 7,000–15,000 people. Districts such as Nyaruguru, Nyamagabe, Nyanza, Kirehe, Gatsibo, Nyagatare Nyabihu and Rutsiro still lag behind with 1 doctor for 25,000–60,000 people. … In total, there are only 87 pharmacists in practice translating to 1 pharmacist per 138,398 population nationally."[126]

There was another failed initiative during the process of making Rwanda a global health model. By 2018, the community-based health insurance system known as Community Based Health Insurance (CBHI)—considered by Kagame, Clinton, and Jim Yong Kim to be a Rwandan innovation to healthcare—was on the verge of collapse. In the words of the auditor-general,

---

[125] See "President Clinton speaks on achievements of Rwanda across all sectors and commits to assisting Rwanda's health sector in becoming free from foreign aid through partnership between the Ministry of Health, Clinton Initiative and 13 top US schools," published on July 20, 2012, https://www.youtube. com/watch?v=oUZWeBjjGc4&feature=youtu.be&list=PLEVvC9V_8948N_YHq7PS4IeHSLZBOWhgC

[126] Republic of Rwanda, Ministry of Health, "Report of Development of Rwanda Master Facility List," November 2018, http://www.moh.gov.rw/fileadmin/user_upload/policies/Validated%20Report%20of%20Rwanda%20Master%20Facility.pdf

> "In order to fully cover the costs of health care for their members, subsidies by the central government and development partners are necessary. ... This current funding mechanism is not able to raise sufficient funds to cover CBHI scheme medical benefits and operational expenditure."[127]

Lastly, neither Kagame nor Jim Yong Kim forgot to return their generosity to Bill Clinton. Kim was to famously credit the Clinton Global Initiative with playing "a catalytic role in international development by bringing together partners who want to make a difference in the world":

> "Whether the goal was to build resilient cities or leverage resources to fight Ebola, the CGI community has changed the way wealth is put to work. ... The CGI community has helped lead the way in recognizing the power of innovative financial tools to bring about significant social impact. ... CGI—using so many tools, including innovative financing—has had great impact on improving the lives of the poorest. I want to thank CGI for all the good it has helped create in the world, especially for all the good it has done for the poor."[128]

Predictably, both the Rwanda government and the World Bank

---

[127] Republic of Rwanda, Auditor General, Report Of The Auditor General Of State Finances For The Year Ended 30 June 2018, http://www.oag.gov.rw/fileadmin/REPORTS/Annual_Report_2018_EXECUTIVE_SUMMARY.pdf

[128] Jim Yong Kim, President of the World Bank, "How the Clinton Global Initiative Changed the Way Wealth is Put to Work," Remarks delivered at the Clinton Global Initiative's 12th and final Annual Meeting," published on Medium by the Clinton Foundation, January 10, 2017, https://stories.clintonfoundation.org/how-the-clinton-global-initiative-changed-the-way-wealth-is-put-to-work-f52f3ff92813

were generous donors to the Clinton Health Access Initiative.[129] Perhaps, no foreign aid episode comes close to the vulgarity displayed by the main characters in the ugly drama of Rwanda's health sector. The operating philosophy seems to have been "you scratch my back and I'll scratch yours," never mind the grandiose claim of transforming Rwanda's healthcare into a global health model envied in Africa and beyond.

---

[129] Clinton Health Access Initiative, Inc., "Cumulative Donations By Donor (January 2010 to March 2019)," Retrieved on August 22, 2019, https://clintonhealthaccess.org/content/uploads/2017/11/CHAI-Donor-List_March-2019.pdf

The Blairs Sought to Build Rwanda State Capacity, Promote Investment, and Provide Legal Support, Not Least Keeping a Rwandan Military General Out of British Jails

Tony Blair and his wife, Cherie Blair, became very close to Kagame, specializing in several fields, including building the capacity of the state, promoting investment, and assisting Rwanda with legal issues. When Tony Blair set up his Africa Governance Initiative (AGI), later changed to the Tony Blair Institute for Global Change, he first experimented with the idea and launched it in Rwanda. The purpose of AGI is explained as follows:

> "AGI was established in 2008 to support leaders in Presidencies and Ministries across Africa to help them turn their visions for development into reality through effective government. This support has helped leaders to bridge the gap between their vision for a better future and their government's ability to implement it. ... The work AGI has supported has been shoulder-to-shoulder and leader-to-leader. ... Over a billion people in Africa need their governments to provide hospitals, schools, sanitation, jobs and much more. When governments

fail to deliver, it's the poor that suffer most. That's why AGI's mission is to support effective governance in Africa—to make government work for the world's poorest people."[130]

AGI describes its work in Rwanda as having developed "a strategic role, supporting the government with their transformational agenda, including a focus on exports diversification in non-traditional sectors such as ICT." In addition, AGI continues to support the Strategic Capacity Building Initiative, which the Tony Blair team "helped to establish, [and] to build its sustainability."[131] In the early phase of AGI's work in Rwanda, which was funded by the British billionaire David Sainsbury, Blair set up a team to work across a range of institutions, including the Executive Office of the President, the Cabinet Secretariat, and the Rwandan Development Board. As Sainsbury's Gatsby Charitable Foundation explains, it supported AGI to build "the capacity and functioning of institutions at the centre of the Rwandan Government. The programme has also supported the Government in developing a broader capacity building strategy."[132]

Meanwhile, Cherie Blair runs various projects in Rwanda including her Foundation for Women that trains women entrepreneurs in the country besides heading an international law firm.[133] Perhaps, Cherie

---

[130] Tony Blair Africa Governance Initiative, "Our mission is to make government work for the world's poorest people," retrieved August 22, 2019, http://www.africagovernance.org/

[131] The Tony Blair Africa Governance Initiative, "Annual Report and Financial Statement," February 28, 2017, http://www.africagovernance.org/pdf/agi-annual-report-2016-2017.pdf

[132] Gatsby Charitable Foundation, "Rwanda Government - We supported the Tony Blair Africa Governance Initiative to help build the capacity and functioning of institutions at the center of the Rwandan Government," retrieved August 28, 2019, https://www.gatsby.org.uk/africa/programmes/rwandan-government

[133] Cherie Blair Foundation for Women, "Accenture awards Cherie Blair Foundation for Women US$1.7 million to help ensure success of women entrepreneurs in Rwanda," March 17, 2014, http://www.cherieblairfoundation.org/accenture-awards-cherie-blair-foundation-for-women-us1-7-million-to-help-ensure-success-of-women-entrepreneurs-in-rwanda/

Blair's most famous association with Kagame involved the arrest of Rwandan spy chief General Karenzi Karake in London in June 2015. The Rwandan general was arrested by the London Metropolitan Police under an international arrest warrant for having ordered civilian massacres, including the killing of Spanish nationals in 1994. In 2008, a Spanish judge indicted Karake for war crimes along with thirty-nine other current or former high-ranking Rwandan military officials. To resist Karenzi's extradition to Spain, Kagame hired Cherie Blair. In no time, Cherie Blair had Karake released on bail of £1 million, and two months later, the general was freed on a legal technicality before the charges could be heard and flew home. Cherie, like her husband, was hailed by Kagame as a hero.[134]

Tony Blair's promotion of foreign investment in Rwanda did not turn out well, however. True, his former strategic advisor at AGI, Guy Baron, is the chief investment officer of Rwanda Development Board (RDB). Back in 2009, for example, Tony jetted to Rwanda to witness the signing of a US$250 million project to produce biofuels from jatropha. The project would see Rwanda growing jatropha on 10,000 hectares of land, from which 20 million liters of biofuel would be extracted annually. The investment was to replace up to 20 percent of Rwandan fossil fuels while creating at least 6,500 jobs. The Kagame government immediately invested in a US$35 million pilot project for testing the process. Kagame was very pleased, announcing on November 14, 2009, that Blair was in Rwanda to view progress in various areas and would "witness the signing of a major green energy investment and visit a biofuel laboratory."[135] Tony Blair was very happy too, stating that Rwanda

---

[134] Mirror, 'Cherie Blair helps get bail for Rwandan spy chief fighting extradition to Spain over alleged war crimes," June 24, 2015, https://www.mirror.co.uk/news/uk-news/cherie-blair-helps-bail-rwandan-5950269; The Telegraph, "Cherie Blair's empire and its secret HQ, The wife of the former prime minister is enjoying her most successful year yet as her law firm and charity both pick up contracts around the world," March 14, 2014, https://www.telegraph.co.uk/news/politics/tony-blair/10732062/Cherie-Blairs-empire-and-its-secret-HQ.html

[135] Paul Kagame, "President Kagame and Tony Blair Renew Relationship – Kigali," 14 November 2009, retrieved on August 22, 2019, http://paulkagame.com/?p=11341

was an innovative state with a leadership that is taking action against climate change:

> "Projects like this are the mark of a truly innovative and pioneering country with a leadership that is not only taking the threat of climate change seriously but taking on the challenge with practical and sustainable solutions. … Whether you want to start a small business or construct a complex multi-million-dollar deal, the Government of Rwanda is serious about helping people do that. With this progressive drive for green investment and clean technology development, Rwanda gives us hope that climate change can be tackled."[136]

The project never saw the light of the day. According to the UK government's Companies House, Eco Positive (Rwanda) Ltd, one of the investors in the project was "dissolved via voluntary strike-off" on October 28, 2014.[137] The pilot project in Rwanda was abandoned in February 2017.[138]

Meanwhile, RDB, whose investment chief is a former Blair's righthand man, Guy Baron, is failing to tame the agency's statistical manipulation. RDB remains a serial liar in this respect. Every year, RDB issues misleading data on foreign investment in Rwanda. Take, for example, the way RDB reported foreign investment in Rwanda in 2018:

---

[136] Tony Blair Globe Institute for Change, "Praise for Paul Kagame During Latest Visit to Rwanda," 16 November 2009, https://institute.global/news/governance/praise-paul-kagame-during-latest-visit-rwanda

[137] UK Government, Companies House, "ECO POSITIVE (RWANDA) LIMITED Company number 07262427," retrieved August 22, 2019, https://beta.companieshouse.gov.uk/company/07262427/filing-history

[138] The East African, "Rwanda abandons $35 million biodiesel pilot project," February 12, 2017, https://www.theeastafrican.co.ke/rwanda/News/Rwanda-abandons-USD35m-biodiesel-pilot-project-/1433218-3808420-8s9a55z/index.html

"The Rwanda Development Board in 2018 registered 173 investment projects in Rwanda worth US$2.006 billion against a US$2 billion target, set for the year. This is an increase of US$331 million or approximately 20%, when compared to the investments registered by RDB in 2017. During 2017, US$ 1.675 billion worth of investments were registered. Of the total investments registered in 2018, an estimated 26% represents export-oriented projects. Across sectors, manufacturing, mining, agriculture and agro-processing accounted for 57% of investments registered. Other sectors that attracted significant investments were tourism, healthcare, business services and ICT."[139]

Reporting "registered" as opposed to foreign investment rendered operational is false reportage designed to impress. As indicated earlier, Rwanda received US$305 million in foreign direct investment in 2018, while the total foreign direct investment stock stands at US$2.2 billion. In other words, RDB is claiming US$2 billion foreign investment registered in a single year, which is equivalent to FDI stock in Rwanda accumulated since 2000 to 2018. Meanwhile, the Blairs are not about to give up assisting Rwanda to attract foreign investment. On September 3, 2019, Cherie Blair headed a delegation comprised of American and British businesspeople to meet Kagame and explore business opportunities in Rwanda.[140]

---

[139] Rwanda Development Board, "Rwanda Development Board registers over US$ 2 billion worth of investments in 2018," January 8, 2019, https://rdb.rw/rwanda-development-board-registers-over-us-2-billion-worth-of-investments-in-2018/

[140] Paul Kagame, "Meeting with Invest Africa US and Mrs. Cherie Blair CBE QC of Omnia Strategy Group," September 9, 2019, https://www.flickr.com/photos/paulkagame/48706469802/

Kagame Built a US$500 Million Business Empire Instead of Unleashing Rwanda's Private Sector to Lead Prosperity-Creation

The business group is known as Crystal Ventures Ltd (CVL). By its own admission, it is the largest business group in Rwanda. As the group explains, CVL "is now the biggest investment company in the country," currently in excess "of 12,000 employees spanning over various industries within Rwanda and other markets."[141] CVL comprises over a dozen companies including, Inyange Industries Ltd in agro-processing, NPD Ltd in construction, Crystal Telecom, Bourbon Coffee in coffee processing, Intersec Ltd in security services, Ruliba Clays Ltd in construction materials, Real Contractors in real-estate development, East African Granite Industries in building materials, Nexus in luxury aircraft chartering services, and CVLD in property-management services. CVL has been a curious subject both in Rwanda

---

[141] Crystal Ventures Ltd, "About Us," retrieved on August 20, 2019, https://www.cvl.co.rw/

and overseas. No less than *The Economist*[142] and *Financial Times*[143] attempted to understand the operations and the size of the group, both estimating CVL to be worth US$500 million in assets. The question is: why does it require estimations to establish the size of Crystal Ventures Ltd in a country that is ranked by the World Bank as the top global performer in terms of institutional transparency and twenty-ninth in the world in terms of business environment?

The reality is that Rwanda fails in every category of OECD's corporate governance, and CVL is proof if any were needed.[144] CVL does not report financial and non-financial information in line with internationally recognized standards of corporate disclosure, including areas of serious concern for the general public and its competitors. CVL issues neither operating results nor its governance, ownership, and voting structure of the enterprise. The remuneration of board members and key executives, board member qualifications, and the selection process are all unknown. Any relevant issues relating to executives, employees, suppliers, and other stakeholders are a mystery. Most revealingly, CVL does not issue annual financial statements. This is all one sees on CVL's website regarding its ownership:

> "We are an investment company established in 1995 in
> Rwanda, initially under the name Tri-Star Investment
> Ltd, before rebranding to our current name in 2009. …

---

[142] The Economist, "Party of business: The Rwandan Patriotic Front's business empire -
Crystal Ventures has investments in everything from furniture to finance," *March 2, 2017,* https://www.economist.com/business/2017/03/02/the-rwandan-patriotic-fronts-business-empire

[143] Financial Times, "Rwandan Patriotic Front: Party builds a formidable business group," September 24, 2012, https://www.ft.com/content/7fcab78c-ff1b-11e1-a4be-00144feabdc0

[144] OECD, "OECD Guidelines on Corporate Governance of State-Owned Enterprises", 2015 Edition, https://www.oecd-ilibrary.org/docserver/9789264244160-en.pdf?expires=1566309104&id=id&accname=guest&checksum=E935F15E3B17353642AC59A934086A88

> The founders were among the pioneers of Rwanda's private sector. … Having made a few good investments, the company earned decent returns that were reinvested to create what is now the biggest investment company in the country. The company's motto—create wealth and improve lives—has spurred the growth of the business whose choice in investment are determined by the opportunity to make a significant impact on the socioeconomic landscape accompanied by the opportunity to venture into explored sectors with high returns in the developing economy."[145]

Occasionally, bits and pieces of information on how CVL operates come to light, not least the fact that the group's largest companies, such as Inyange Industries and the East African Granite Industries, were built with Rwandan workers' pension funds. Some of this information is often revealed unwittingly when the ruling party newspaper, *The New Times*, when showcasing Kagame's grand achievements. For example, in its article titled "Kagame unveils model granite factory," *The New Times* exposed the sources of financing for CVL's East African Granite Industries to be Rwanda's pension fund:

> "President Paul Kagame yesterday officially opened East African Granite Industries (EAGI), currently the largest in the region. Built on 72 hectares in Nyagatare district in the eastern province, the US$15 million factory was constructed through a joint venture between Crystal Ventures and Rwanda Social Security Board."[146]

The numerous government projects awarded to CVL companies are sometimes revealed by the group's entities themselves. NPD Ltd, for example, thrives on government contracts, which include dam

---

[145] Crystal Ventures Ltd, Ibid.

[146] The New Times, "Kagame unveils model granite factory," July 7, 2012, https://www.newtimes.co.rw/section/read/54814

construction, road construction, building stadiums, bridge construction, highway lighting, and construction of high-voltage transmission lines. These are some of the government projects awarded to NPD Ltd:

1. "Rwanda Transport Development Agency (RTDA) awarded NPD LTD an annual tender to do the periodic maintenance of existing asphalt roads along Crete Congo Nil-Ntendezi Road (31km)-NR 10 in Rusizi and Nyamasheke District."

2. "Rwanda Civil Aviation Authority has awarded NPD LTD an annual tender to do the maintenance works for the runway apron, taxiways and all service roads at the Kigali International Airport, Kamembe Airport and Gisenyi Airport."

3. "The City of Kigali Under the Rwanda Ministry of Infrastructure (MININFRA) awarded NPD LTD a tender of maintaining all asphalt roads in the city of Kigali for a better road network in the city."

4. "NPD LTD wins new lucrative contracts from Electricity Distribution Corporation Limited, EDCL."

5. "The ministry of trade and industry (MINICOM) has awarded NPD LTD a project of constructing 7km of Asphalt road in Bugesera District with the finishing layer made of Asphalt concrete."

6. "It is yet another tender NPD LTD won from the Rwanda Transport Development Agency (RTDA) of upgrading 63km of existing earth road connecting three districts."[147]

The case of how Kagame charters executive jets from Crystal Ventures Ltd came to light from various sources, including the Panama Papers and the Rwandan government's response. The Panama Papers identified Brigadier General Emmanuel Ndahiro, a Kagame confidant, who served as the president's physician, security adviser, and intelligence chief as a director of British Virgin Islands company Debden Investments Limited, which owned a jet aircraft. Interestingly,

---

[147] NPD, "Ongoing projects," retrieved on 20 August 2019, https://npd.co.rw/category/ongoing-projects/

Ndahiro listed a commercial section of a West London neighborhood as his address. Another director in Debben was Hatari Sekoko, a former Rwandan Patriotic Front fighter and now a leading businessman in Rwanda closely associated with Kagame.[148] In the official reaction to the Panama Papers, the government did not deny the existence of the aircraft. Finance Minister Claver Gatete responded as follows: an offshore company mentioned in the Panama papers was established in 1998 "as a special purpose vehicle to secure strategic services," which included "the lease of a secure and convenient mode of transportation for Government leaders."[149] *The Financial Times* also reported that Crystal Ventures Ltd "bought two executive jets, which it then leased to—among others—President Kagame."[150] A South African investigative report came to the same conclusion, revealing the extraordinary length to which the Kagame government sought to mask the ownership of the aircraft.[151]

As bad as the CVL state capture sounds, there is an even more corrupt state–private interest relationship in Kagame's Rwanda, namely, Prime Holdings Ltd. Back in September 2005, the Kagame government failed to publish the audit of Prime Holdings, as per *Memorandum of Economic and Financial Policies* with the IMF. At the time, Prime Holdings was building and managing public properties, including two

---

[148] Panama Papers, "Rwanda: Emmanuel Ndahiro, Brigadier General (2015-present); Chief of the intelligence agency in Rwanda (2004-2011)," https://www.icij.org/investigations/panama-papers/the-power-players/

[149] Claver Gatete, Minister of Finance, "Comment by Minister of Finance to Rwanda mention in Panama Papers", 6 April 2016, http://www.minecofin.gov.rw/index.php?id=12&L=ftp%3A%2F%2F2015julho%3Aeueu2301%40ftp.uhserver.com%2Fteste.php%3F%3F&tx_ttnews%5Btt_news%5D=495&cHash=9314222841246ab80f9fe1a8308329f0

[150] Financial Times, "Rwandan Patriotic Front: Party builds a formidable business," September 24, 2012, https://www.ft.com/content/7fcab78c-ff1b-11e1-a4be-00144feabdc0

[151] De Wet Potgierter and Raymond Joseph, Sunday Times, "Rwanda splurges on luxury jets, February 14, 2010, https://www.timeslive.co.za/sunday-times/lifestyle/2010-02-14-rwanda-splurges-on-luxury-jets/

major hotels. The government then requested a waiver for the non-observance of a September deadline, submitting the audit in December 2005. The IMF concluded that Rwanda's adherence to "conditionality was poor" because the "Prime Holdings' audit was not met." But even when the audit was published, the situation did not improve. According to the IMF, "as the audit found serious shortcomings, the contract with the management of both hotels under Prime Holdings was terminated." The Kagame government informed the IMF that the government had terminated Prime Holdings:

> "With a view to enhancing transparency related to Prime Holdings' two hotels, we have published a financial audit and business plan of Prime Holdings in December 2005 (missed end-September performance criterion). As the auditors concluded that "it was not possible to determine if proper books of account were kept by the hotels", we have canceled the contract with the management company and are in negotiations with the Intercontinental group to take on the management of the hotels."[152]

Fast forward to 2016, when the government launched the Kigali Convention Center (KCC), built with the proceeds from the US$400 million Eurobond.[153] The government now announced that KCC "is owned by multiple stakeholders, including Crystal Ventures Limited, the Government through Prime Holdings, Rwanda Social Security

---

[152] IMF, "Rwanda: Sixth Review Under the Three-Year Arrangement Under the Poverty Reduction and Growth Facility (PRGF), Requests for Waivers of Non-observance of Performance Criteria", July 2006, https://www.imf.org/external/pubs/ft/scr/2006/cr06245.pdf

[153] Republic of Rwanda, Ministry of Finance and Economic Planning, "Rwanda's $400 million Eurobond named 2013 Deal of the Year by Euromoney, February 25, 2014, http://www.minecofin.gov.rw/index.php?id=12&tx_ttnews%5Btt_news%5D=161&cHash=84cafde2e62af961ff9b79a93e82f7f9

Board (RSSB) and Rwanda Investment Group (RIG)."[154] How the ruling party's Crystal Ventures Ltd came to co-own KCC is a mystery. How Prime Holdings, which the government shut down in 2006 in the interest of "transparency," resurfaced to co-own a public entity for which Rwandans went into debt to the tune of US$400 million is another mystery. This is quite simply corruption. In this environment of state capture, it becomes easier to explain why the private sector fails in Rwanda: because each sector is dominated by a powerful interest. Here, we see a situation where a powerful ruler, using party and state institutions, builds a business empire that benefits private interests. As various studies of state capture have shown, in extreme cases such as Rwanda, public institutions such as the legislature, the executive, the judiciary, and regulatory agencies are subject to capture. State capture in Rwanda, therefore, means that unregulated influence of a single interest group bends state laws, policies, and regulations at free will, without any counterbalancing checks. Rwanda becomes a special case because its constitution gives powers to the president to appoint and dismiss everybody across the three branches of government as follows:

> "4° appointment and dismissal of the following judges and prosecutors: a) the President, Vice President and Judges of the Supreme Court; b) the President and Vice President of the High Court, and the President and Vice President of the Commercial High Court; c) the Prosecutor General and the Deputy Prosecutor General.
>
> 5° appointment and dismissal of the following officials: a) the Director of Cabinet in the Office of the President of the Republic; b) Chairpersons, Vice Chairpersons and other Commissioners of national commissions, Heads and Deputy Heads of Government specialised organs, public institutions and parastatals with legal personality;

---

[154] Bryan Kimenyi, The New Times, "Kagame launches Kigali Convention Centre", July 8, 2016, https://www.newtimes.co.rw/section/read/201523

c) Heads and Deputy Heads of Public Universities and institutions of higher learning; d) the Principal Private Secretary to the President of the Republic; e) Advisers in the Office of the President; f) Heads of services in the Office of the President; g) Clerks of Parliament and their Deputies, Secretary General of the Supreme Court, Secretary General of the National Public Prosecution Authority ...

6° The Prime Minister is selected, appointed and dismissed by the President of the Republic. Other Cabinet members are appointed by the President of the Republic."[155]

And as shown earlier, the current Rwandan constitution immunizes Kagame from criminality even after he leaves office. With the Rwandan state so utterly captured, who will dare tell Kagame not to corruptly give government contracts to Crystal Ventures Ltd for the sake of building a competitive private sector in Rwanda? No one. On the contrary, Kagame has, over the years, illegally seized domestic and foreign companies without compensation. Perhaps the most famous cases involved the US multinational company Chevron and the local company Union Trade Centre (UTC), owned by a Rwandan pan-African businessman Tribert Rujugiro Ayabatwa. The Chevron case was described by the United States embassy officials in Kigali, courtesy of Wikileaks, which shared the confidential report:

> "On July 1, Chevron closed shop in Rwanda. Citing extensive fraud in its Rwandan operations ... Chevron decided last November to stop doing business in the country. The U.S. oil company quietly handed over its operations to Saudi firm Bakri International, and will pull out its remaining two expatriate employees in the next few weeks. Chevron executives assert the

---

[155] Republic of Rwanda, Rwandan Constitution, Ibid.

> GOR is stonewalling on a promise to reimburse them for a fuel storage tank Chevron installed in Kigali's Gregoire Kayibanda international airport in May 2008. Rwanda can ill afford to lose high profile investors like Chevron especially as it tries to overcome its reputation as a difficult place to do business. Despite aggressive marketing, Rwanda has failed to attract new investment from first-tier multinationals. Chevron's withdrawal, however discrete, also raises questions about the country's supposedly squeaky-clean record on corruption."[156]

Bakri International did not last either. The company mysteriously lost its business to its local representative, Egide Gatera, who re-emerged as the proprietor of Société Pétrolière sarl (SP), which took over the business after its Saudi owners lost a futile court case in Rwanda's Commercial High Court.[157] In the UTC case, The Kagame government illegally seized UTC in 2013 and took over its management, claiming that the business was abandoned because Ayabatwa resided outside Rwanda. In 2015, the very government that had seized the business claimed UTC owed taxes amounting to US$1.4 million. The regime seemed to have forgotten it was the one managing the company for two years. And then, on September 25, 2017, the government auctioned the UTC for a mere US$8 million.[158]

---

[156] See Classified By: Charge Cheryl Sim, "Chevron Pulls Out of Rwanda", August 13, 2008, CONFIDENTIAL, https://www.wikileaks.org/plusd/cables/08KIGALI558_a.html

[157] See Rwanda Commercial High Court, "Société Pétrolière sarl (SP) C/ BAKRI INTERNATIONAL ENERGY Co (Rwanda) Ltd (Bakri Rwanda) R COM A 0214/10/HCC 04/08/2010, http://197.243.16.111/judiciary/uploads/tx_publications/R%20COM%20A%200214-10-HCC%20SP%20v%20BAKRI%20RWANDA%20et%20csrts.pdf

[158] Mfonobong Nsehe, Forbes, "Rwandan Tobacco Millionaire Tribert Rujugiro Loses Shopping Mall to Government," Sep 29, 2017 https://www.forbes.com/sites/mfonobongnsehe/2017/09/29/rwandan-government-auctions-shopping-mall-owned-by-tobacco-millionaire/#3cbf083522ab

On Paper, Rwanda Received US$20.8 Billion Foreign Aid in 1994-2020. Where Did the Money Go?

Rwanda is addicted to foreign aid. With official development assistance per capita at US$102, Rwanda is the highest foreign-aid recipient in East Africa, except for war-torn South Sudan. Rwanda received US$17.2 billion in foreign aid between 1994 and 2017. And based on the current trend of receiving US$1.2 billion a year, Rwanda will have received US$3.6 billion in 2018–2020. That means, therefore, that Rwanda received US$20.8 billion in foreign aid from 1994 to 2020. Table 7 shows the amount of foreign aid to Rwanda from 1994 to 2017.

As shown in table 7, annual foreign aid to Rwanda during the Kagame era began at US$771.7 million in 1994 and was, at the time, focused on emergency relief associated with the genocide. The emergency phase of foreign aid to Rwanda ended in 2000, giving way to development assistance. Foreign aid to Rwanda began to increase sharply, reaching US$491 million in a single year in 2004 and hitting the billion-dollar mark in 2010. Foreign aid to Rwanda fell back to below the billion mark in 2012.

Table 7. Foreign aid to Rwanda, 1994–2017 (millions in US$)

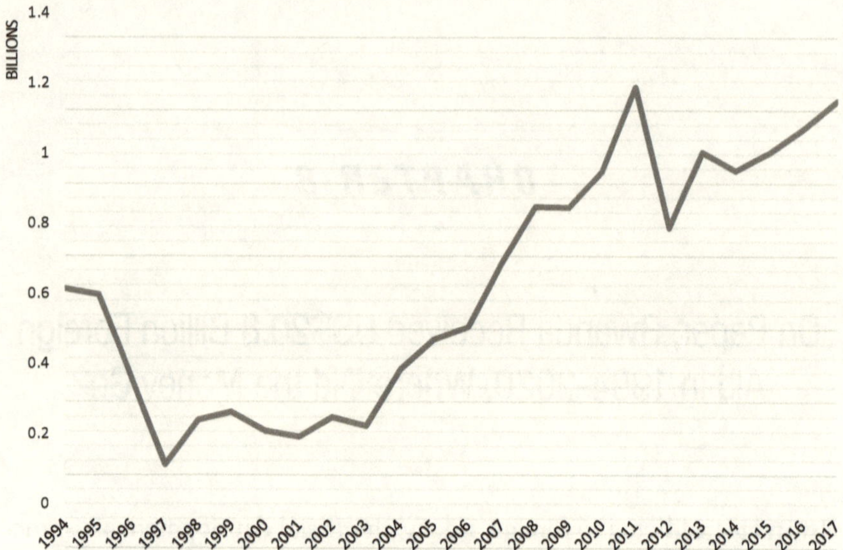

Source: World Bank, Official Development Assistance (ODA) database, 2018

This was when donors sought to punish Kagame by either suspending or cutting off their support for his sponsorship of armed militias in the Democratic Republic of Congo. The Kagame-donor relationship improved a year later, with foreign aid to Rwanda once again rising above the million-dollar mark. In 2017, foreign aid reached US$1.2 billion.[159]

Regarding the ranking of foreign aid donors to Rwanda, the World Bank's International Development Association (IDA) tops the list, followed by the United States, the European Union, the International Monetary Fund (IMF), and the United Kingdom. The Global Fund, the African Development Fund, the Netherlands, Germany, and Japan complete the list of Rwanda's top-ten aid givers. Table 8 on Rwanda's top-ten donors indicates the aid-giver and the amount received, on average, in 2016 and 2017.

---

[159] OECD, "Aid Receipts for Rwanda," https://public.tableau.com/views/ OECDDACAidataglancebyrecipient_new/Recipients?:embed=y&:display count=yes&:showTabs=y&:toolbar=no?&:showVizHome=no.

Table 8. Rwanda's top-ten donors, 2016–2017 average (US$ million)

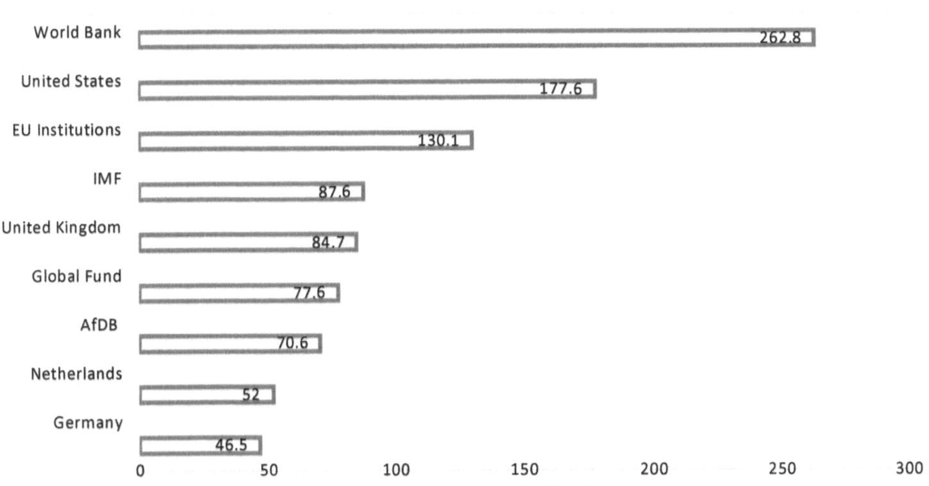

Source: OECD, Aid database, Receipts for Rwanda, 2017

Of the US$1.2 billion in foreign aid to Rwanda in 2017, the World Bank's share was US$262.8 million, followed by the United States at US$177.6 million, European Union institutions at US$130.1 million, the International Monetary Fund at US$87.6 million, the United Kingdom at US$84.7 million, the Global Fund at US$77.6 million, the African Development Bank at US$70.6 million, the Netherlands at US$52 million, Germany at US$46.5 million, and Japan at US$35.6 million. The United States and the United Kingdom were Rwanda's first- and second-largest bilateral aid donors, respectively, as has been the case over the past two decades.

The World Bank's lead in financing Rwanda may be illustrated by the amounts of concessional loans provided by the International Development Association (IDA) between 2009 and 2019. In this phase, the World Bank alone spent US$2.8 billion in Rwanda.[160] Table 9 shows

---

[160] The World Bank, Rwanda, Projects and Operations, http://projects.worldbank. org/search?lang=en&searchTerm=&countrycode_exact=RW

how the modest amount of US$26.5 million in World Bank financing in 2009 sharply rose to more than half a billion by 2018, dropping slightly to US$452.3 million in 2019. Under Jim Yong Kim's presidency from 2012 to 2019, the World Bank was very generous indeed to Kim's friend Kagame.

Table 9. World Bank aid to Rwanda, 2009–2019 (millions in US$)

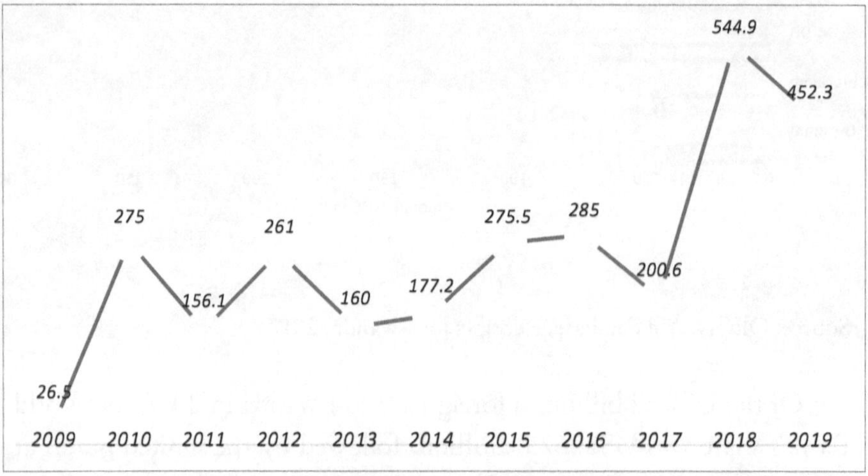

Source: World Bank database, Rwanda Projects and Operations

Regarding the sectors supported by bilateral foreign aid in Rwanda, in 2017, for example, 24 percent went into health, 19 percent into other social infrastructure, 15 percent into production, 14 percent into economic infrastructure, 11 percent into education, 7 percent into humanitarian support, and the rest into multisector actions.[161] Bilateral aid sector support is shown in table 10.

---

[161] OECD, Receipts for Rwanda, 2016-2017, https://public.tableau.com/views/ OECDDACAidataglancebyrecipient_new/Recipients?:embed=y&:display_ count=yes&:showTabs=y&:toolbar=no?&:showVizHome=no

Table 10. Bilateral aid to Rwanda by sector, 2017 (%)

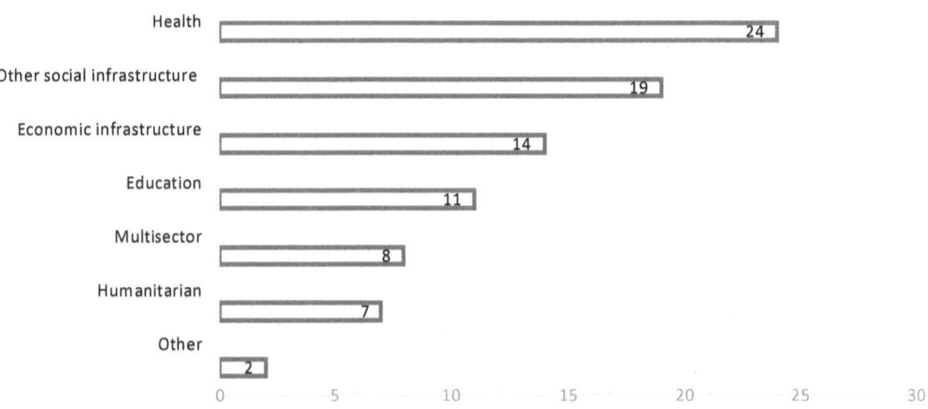

Source: OECD, Aid database, Receipts for Rwanda, 2017

The most intriguing question is where the foreign aid of US$20.8 billion to Rwanda went. To illustrate, let us look at the electricity sector. Donor financing of the Rwandan energy sector between 2009 and 2019 was intense. Begin with US$357 million contributed in 2009 by the World Bank, the African Development Bank (AfDB), the Arab Bank for Economic Development in Africa (BADEA), Belgium, the European Union (EU), the Netherlands, Japan, the OPEC Fund for International Development (OFID), and the Saudi Fund. [162] The European Union put in €200 million, or US$224.9 million, for sustainable energy in 2014–2020.[163] The World Bank gave US$125 million in 2018 to the energy sector.[164] The African Development Bank put into the sector

---

[162] World Bank, "Rwanda Electricity Access Scale-up Project (P111567)," closing date of 30-Mar-2018 http://documents.worldbank.org/curated/en/102241553114033231/pdf/Rwanda-Rwanda-Electricity-Access-Scale-up-Proj.pdf

[163] European Union, "European Union-Republic of Rwanda National Indicative Program for the Period 2014-2020," https://ec.europa.eu/europeaid/sites/devco/files/pin-rwanda-fed11-2014_en.pdf

[164] World Bank, "Second Rwanda Energy Sector Development Policy Financing," October 19, 2018, Http://Documents.Worldbank.Org/Curated/En/370591542596427420/Pdf/Rwanda-Pad-10252018-636781752161979044.Pdf

€229.20 million, or US$257.7 million, in 2019.[165] Add US$120 million from the World Bank for skills development that targeted the energy sector, among others.[166] Donors, therefore, spent US$1 billion in the Rwandan energy sector in ten years between 2009 and 2019. Here is the World Bank assessment of Rwanda's energy sector in 2019:

> "Despite recent progress, Rwanda's cost of electricity service delivery is among the highest in the region (around US$0.28/kWh in FY2017/18), and tariffs are barely enough to cover operating cost of the utility, Rwanda Electricity Group (REG). The Government of Rwanda has been stepping in to fill the gap between sector cost and revenues and provide grants for capital expenditure. Electricity subsidies are budgeted at 1.4 percent of GDP in FY2017/18 and at 1.5 percent of GDP for FY2018/19. Plans for rapid system expansion during NST1, already only possible at relatively high costs due to country's lack of low-cost domestic energy resources, carried significant fiscal risks because (a) contracts with private developers to develop capacity were procured through bilaterally negotiated deals rather than competitive procurement; (b) the country prioritized costlier domestic sources over cheaper supply from neighboring countries (e.g., Ethiopia, Kenya, or Uganda); (c) investment planning was inconsistent with least-cost planning principles; and (d) there is

---

[165] African Development Bank, "Rwanda and African Development Bank sign €229 million loan agreements to finance electricity projects," October 17, 2018, https://www.afdb.org/en/news-and-events/rwanda-and-african-development-bank-sign-eur229-million-loan-agreements-to-finance-electricity-projects-18584

[166] World Bank, "Rwanda Priority Skills for Growth (PSG) (P252350)," Archived September 28, 2018, http://documents.worldbank.org/curated/en/231621543944759171/pdf/Disclosable-Version-of-the-ISR-Rwanda-Priority-Skills-for-Growth-PSG-P252350-Sequence-No-03.pdf

limited scope for tariff increases as electricity is already unaffordable for much of the population."[167]

This is a catastrophe. The Rwandan electricity sector is in a mess, as further confirmed by the auditor-general, who described the sector in 2018 as follows:

> "The country continues to face a problem of expensive power from Thermal power plants and yet majority of Hydro power plants are operating below installed power production capacity. Out of the existing 27 hydro power plants at 30 June 2017, only six (6) power plants operated at more than 50% of their installed power production capacity. Nine (9) plants operated between 30% and 40 % while other seven (7) plants operated below 25% of their installed power production capacity. The remaining five (5) power plants had not generated electricity during the year."[168]

The most spectacular failure involved the 15-megawatt Gishoma power plant, which cost RWF40,570,617,811, or US$44.1 million. Construction of the power plant began in February 2013 and was expected to end in May 2014 but was completed in 2017. What happened next is described by the auditor-general:

> "The power plant stopped production activities on 27 September 2017 after only 4 months of operations. This was due to the lack of enough quantity and quality of peat and insufficient supply of water and the breakdown

---

[167] World Bank, "Second Rwanda Energy Sector Development Policy Financing (P166458)," 03-May-2018, http://documents.worldbank.org/curated/en/336541527006749374/pdf/Concept-Program-Information-Document-PID-Second-Rwanda-Energy-Sector-Development-Policy-Operation-P166458.pdf

[168] Republic of Rwanda, Auditor General, "Report of The Auditor General of State Finances for the Year Ended 30 June 2018, http://www.oag.gov.rw/fileadmin/REPORTS/Annual Report 2018 EXECUTIVE SUMMARY.pdf

in some parts of installed machinery. The continued stoppage of the power plant implies that envisaged electricity supply requirements are not being served during the period of stoppage. As such, there may be no value for money realized from this investment."[169]

The national electricity company, Rwanda Energy Group (REG), was barely functional:

"REG and Subsidiaries (EUCL and EDCL) with total assets of Frw 454,356,991,835 as at 30 June 2015 [US$494.2 million] had no books of account to support the financial statements and hence no proper accountability for their operations for the year ended 30 June 2015. The financial statements for the year ended 30 June 2016 had not been prepared and submitted to the Auditor General's office by 31st December 2016."[170]

Meanwhile, REG is kept afloat by annual government grants of US$16 million, as was the case in 2017 and 2018.[171] In a 2019 internal report, REG indicates that Rwanda's electricity sector is tiny, with 221.9 megawatts installed as opposed to 154.1 megawatts available:

"Rwanda's national power system is still small. Despite its high growth rate …, annual addition of the generating

---

[169] Republic of Rwanda, Auditor General, Report of The Auditor General of State Finances for the Year Ended 30 June 2017, http://www.oag.gov.rw/fileadmin/user_upload/Financial_Reports/ANNUAL_REPORT_JUNE_2017_EXECUTIVE_SUMMARY.pdf

[170] Republic of Rwanda, Auditor General, Report of The Auditor General of State Finances for the Year Ended 30 June 2016, http://www.oag.gov.rw/fileadmin/user_upload/Financial_Reports/ANNUAL_REPORT_JUNE_2016_EXECUTIVE_SUMMARY.pdf

[171] Energy Utility Corporation Ltd, "Annual Report and Financial Statements for the Year Ended 30 June 2018, http://www.reg.rw/fileadmin/user_upload/EUCL_FINANCIAL_STATEMENTS_FOR_2017_2018.pdf

capacity required to expand the system is still very small. This reduces the ability of the electricity sector to benefit from economies of scale through construction of new large generating units."[172]

So, where did the US$1 billion foreign aid money targeting the electricity sector from 2009 to 2019 go? Let us take a closer look at the US$120 million skills development loan that targeted the energy sector, among others. The program of actions included the following tasks:

- Provide advice on change management to the heads of the institutions that will undergo restructuring;
- Train a cadre of project-management staff to better understand best practices, procedures, and systems;
- Engage technical expertise in the areas of curriculum, pedagogy, assessment, ICT, and management;
- Upgrade the quality and number of instructors at the TVET level;
- Increase capacity in quality assurance and regulation of institutions;
- Partner with an international apex institution to understand the role of an apex body;
- Develop and operate a student-loan MIS;
- Develop an M&E system to be undertaken considering multiple agencies;
- Strengthen inspection and monitoring of tertiary institutions.

Embarrassingly, almost all these tasks in the US$120 million loan were done by external consultants, including the preparation of skills inception report. The World Bank admits as much:

---

[172] REG, "Rwanda Least Cost Power Development Plan (LCPDP) 2019 – 2040," June 2019, http://www.reg.rw/fileadmin/user_upload/LCPDP_REPORT_June_2019.pdf

"Rwanda Development Board Chief Skills Officer (RDB-CSO) has now contracted an external firm, Dalberg, to support preparation of the National Skills Development and Employment Promotion Strategy (NSDEPS). Relevant stakeholder consultations on the inception report are ongoing. RDB-CSO is to encourage to consider a more realistic timeline for preparing NSDEPS, so as to ensure adequate quality assurance of the Strategy by a small technical group constituted for the purpose."[173]

Another issue with foreign aid to Rwanda is the low absorption capacity in the ministries, departments, and agencies (MDAs). To illustrate, let us look at the African Development Bank's financing of the energy sector between 2013 and 2017, summed up in table 11.

Table 11. Foreign Aid–funded energy projects at risk due to low absorption capacity

Project	Foreign aid ($)	Expected outcome	Status
1. Installation of Low Voltage and Medium Voltage lines and service connections in Burera, Musanze, and Gakenke districts	US$6,343,921.33, funded by the African Development Fund	Construction begun on July 2015, to be completed in June 2017	Uncompleted and terminated on 10 March 2017

---

[173] World Bank, Rwanda Priority Skills for Growth (PSG) (P252350), Implementation Status & Results Report, ARCHIVED on 22-Apr-2019, http://documents.worldbank.org/curated/en/437641555948196411/pdf/Disclosable-Version-of-the-ISR-Rwanda-Priority-Skills-for-Growth-PSG-P252350-Sequence-No-04.pdf

2.	93.2 km transmission line of 220 KV between Shango substation, Gasabo district, and Uganda border	US$14,850,866 funded by African Development Fund	Construction begun in November 2013, to be completed in June 2015	Not operational by December 2017
3.	179.6 km transmission line system of 220 KV, Karongi-Rubavu-Kigali-Goma	US$26,386,234.89 funded by African Development Fund	Construction begun in November 2013, to be completed in November 2015	Not operational by December 2017
4.	Substations of 220 KV transmission system, Kibuye (Karongi)-Gisenyi (Rubavu)-Goma –Kigali	US$11,567,214 and €7,430,437 funded by African Development Fund	Construction began in November 2013, to be completed in April 2015	Abandoned and uncompleted by December 2017
5.	Electrification project in Ngororero district:	US$ 11,807,266 funded by the African Development Fund	Construction began in November 2013, to be completed in September 2017	Electrical lines did not transmit electricity by December 2017

Source: *Auditor-General Report*, 2017[174]

---

[174] Republic of Rwanda, "Report of The Auditor General of State Finances for the Year Ended 30 June 2017," http://www.oag.gov.rw/fileadmin/user_upload/Financial_Reports/ANNUAL_REPORT_JUNE_2017_EXECUTIVE_SUMMARY.pdf

As indicated in table 11, the African Development Bank (AfDB), through the African Development Fund, financed Rwanda's energy projects to the tune of nearly US$80 million, all of which remained at risk at the end of 2017. By 2018, the situation had worsened considerably. The auditor-general indicated that RWF 136,247,858,326, or US$148 million, was at risk of being reclaimed by donors because the projects' closing dates were approaching while funds remained undrawn. As the auditor-general further explained:

> "There are instances where contracts are either delayed, abandoned or subsequently terminated. Hence low project funds absorption. These funds are at risk of being forfeited by Government and the intended objectives of the projects may not be realized."[175]

Attempting to understand where US$20.8 billion in foreign aid to Rwanda went echoes Dambisa Moyo's book *Dead Aid*. As she reasoned, more than US$1 trillion in foreign aid was transferred to Africa in the past fifty years. Moyo asked and answered her own question as follows: "Has this assistance improved the lives of Africans? No. In fact, across the continent, the recipients of this aid are not better off as a result of it, but worse—much worse." [176] And so, it is with Rwanda. The US$20.8 billion foreign aid to Rwanda is largely besides the point for millions of Rwandans, especially those who live in rural areas. There, food security, electricity, all-weather roads, and piped water have yet to arrive in their villages, the US$20.8 billion in foreign aid to Rwanda notwithstanding.

---

[175] Republic of Rwanda, "Report of The Auditor General of State Finances for the Year Ended 30 June 2018," http://www.oag.gov.rw/fileadmin/REPORTS/Annual_Report_2018_EXECUTIVE_SUMMARY.pdf

[176] Dambisa Moyo, *Dead Aid*, http://dambisamoyo.com/publications-articles-videos/books/dead-aid/

A US$200 Million World Bank Loan Is Building 14,680 Latrines, Among Other Things, as a Means of Kickstarting Rwanda's Human Capital Development

At the World Bank's 2018 annual meetings plenary, Jim Yong Kim credited Kagame with helping him to persuade the World Bank to prioritize human capital development. As Kim put it, "At the last Annual Meetings, President Paul Kagame helped make the case for human capital." [177] Kim was referring to his invitation to Kagame in 2017 to deliver the keynote address at the launch of the World Bank's human capital development project. Kagame's keynote address included the following rhetoric:

> "Human capital is without doubt the driver of high-income growth and the foundation of prosperity. This is not an abstraction. We are talking about people in real terms. ... As we worked to rebuild the nation, we had no choice but to put our people at the center of our strategy. ... Human capital generates prosperity

[177] Jim Yong Kim, "Remarks by World Bank Group President Jim Yong Kim at the 2018 Annual Meetings Plenary," October 12, 2018, HTTPS://WWW. WORLDBANK.ORG/EN/NEWS/SPEECH/2018/10/12/REMARKS-BY-WORLD-BANK-GROUP-PRESIDENT-JIM-YONG-KIM-AT-THE-2018-ANNUAL-MEETINGS-PLENARY

by enabling mindsets of responsibility, productivity, innovation, and self-reliance. We are very happy to work with the World Bank Group and other partners to ensure that this perspective remains at the top of the sustainable development agenda."[178]

The World Bank would later state that "President Kagame is Global Champion for the Human Capital Project and the Government is part of the early adopter program."[179] Kim's choice of Kagame to deliver the keynote address on human capital development and to make the Rwandan ruler the global champion of the program was peculiar. The World Bank's Human Capital Index rankings show why this choice was inexplicable. Rwanda is in the bottom quantile with a ranking of 142nd out of 157 countries. Rwanda's ranking is below the average of both the sub-Saharan African region and low-income economies.[180] Asking Kagame to champion human capital is like designating a failing student a leader of a class that includes top performers. What was going on here? This incomprehensible relationship between Kagame and Kim led to Rwanda's acquisition of a US$200 million World Bank loan aimed at building the foundation for human capital development. The loan is to address the education shambles in Rwanda through three program components.[181]

---

[178] Paul Kagame, "Address by President Kagame at the Human Capital Summit – World Bank Group Annual Meetings," October 13, 2017, retrieved September 10, 2019, http://paulkagame.com/?p=11829

[179] Kristalina Georgieva, "The future drivers of growth in Rwanda," December 18, 2018, HTTPS://BLOGS.WORLDBANK.ORG/NASIKILIZA/THE-FUTURE-DRIVERS-OF-GROWTH-IN-RWANDA

[180] World Bank, "Rwanda Human Capital Index," 2017, https://databank.worldbank.org/data/download/hci/HCI_2pager_RWA.pdf

[181] World Bank, "Project Appraisal Document on a Proposed Credit in The Amount ff SDR 145.2 Million (US$200.0 Million) to the Republic of Rwanda for the Rwanda Quality Basic Education for Human Capital Development Project," July 9, 2019 http://documents.worldbank.org/curated/en/184411564797693303/pdf/Rwanda-Quality-Basic-Education-for-Human-Capital-Development-Project.pdf

Component 1, costed at US$46.6 million, aims at enhancing "teacher effectiveness for improved student learning." This includes (a) improving teachers' English language proficiency and digital skills, (b) supporting professional development of mathematics and science teachers, (c) strengthening preparation of new teachers, and (d) developing model schools to support innovative instructional practices. Component 2, costed at US$126 million, will improve "the school environment to support student learning." This component aims to (a) reduce overcrowding and distance to schools, (b) enrich early learning environment, and (c) support gender-sensitive teaching and learning environments. Component 3, costed at US$13 million, aims at "developing institutional capacity to strengthen teaching and learning." This is subdivided into (a) supporting quality assurance systems, and (b) strengthening project management, implementation, and monitoring capacity.[182]

Component 1 makes sense. As the 2019 World Bank's diagnostic analysis indicated, the magnitude of Rwanda's education challenge is enormous. "Learning outcomes are alarmingly low: only 45 percent of 2nd and 5th graders tested in 2014 met grade level expectations in Kinyarwanda and in English; and the average score for mathematics was 33 percent for 2nd graders and 38 percent for 5th graders." Qualified teachers of English and mathematics are rare. Improving Rwandan teachers' English language proficiency is long overdue. Previous attempts failed since Kagame overnight switched the teaching language in Rwanda from French to English in 2008.

The most problematic parts of the US$200 million education project are components 2 and 3. In the case of component 2, which aims to reduce overcrowding and distance to schools, the project "will finance the construction of 11,000 furnished classrooms and approximately

---

[182] World Bank, "Project Appraisal Document on a Proposed Credit in The Amount of SDR 145.2 Million (US$200.0 Million)," Ibid.

14,680 latrines."[183] The bulk of the US$200 million, namely, US$126 will build the classrooms and latrines. This is most embarrassing. Kagame has been boasting that Rwanda is ready to end its dependency on foreign aid. But here he is receiving foreign aid to build 14,680 latrines. How can a ruler who says he has built an African economic lion fail to build latrines? The answer is simple. Most school buildings and environments in Rwanda remain structurally unsafe and hazardous. Sanitary facilities across the country are rare, while primary school classrooms house more than eighty pupils, with five sharing a desk. The toilet situation, however, is an utter disgrace, an issue that the auditor-general publicized in a 2016 report on uncompleted and abandoned school infrastructure. The problem was what he termed "unconventional construction methods," whereby the government "is supplying part of the materials and another part is supplied by the schools themselves in collaboration with the sectors." In other words, the central government abandoned the school infrastructure development it had launched in 2009. When in February-March 2016, the auditor-general conducted site reviews in four districts (Gasabo, Rusizi, Nyamagabe, Nyagatare), he found ninety-three latrines and three classrooms abandoned. On the same subject, the Ministry of Education stated in 2017 that "the number of users per toilet has remained constant at 57 for students, while it has worsened for staff from 11 users per toilet in 2016 to 27 in 2017."[184]

Sadly, while building latrines and classrooms will consume US$126 million, the education project is silent on the improvement of teachers' well-being. As shown earlier, a primary school teacher in Rwanda earns less than US$1.90 a day and is, therefore, trapped in poverty. Then, there is the question of who might build the infrastructure in this US$200 million education project. Some fear that Kagame's Crystal Ventures

---

[183] World Bank, "Project Appraisal Document on a Proposed Credit in The Amount of SDR 145.2 Million (US$200.0 Million)," Ibid.

[184] Republic of Rwanda, Ministry of Education, "2017 Rwanda Education Statistics", 2018, http://www.mineduc.gov.rw/fileadmin/user_upload/pdf_files/Rwanda_Education_Statistics_2017.pdf

Ltd might either emerge as the contractor of the classrooms and latrines or sell building materials to the contractors. Lastly, component 3 of the education project costed at US$13.5 million, will be spent on enhancing

> "early learning by pre-primary and lower primary school-age children through the development of engaging educational entertainment content to supplement learning in classrooms. These materials will be accessible through radio, TVs, and phones for children, parents, and teachers in school and at home."[185]

There is one major problem here: 84 percent of Rwandan rural households do not have electricity, let alone a television.

---

[185] World Bank, "Project Appraisal Document on a Proposed Credit in The Amount ff SDR 145.2 Million (US$200.0 Million) to the Republic of Rwanda for the Rwanda Quality Basic Education for Human Capital Development Project," Op. Cit.

CHAPTER 10

Kagame Closed the Border Through Which Much of Rwanda's US$3 Billion Annual International Trade Transits Shortly After Being Suspended from US Trade Facilitation

Rwanda is a weak trader. As indicated earlier, a 2019 study by the World Bank indicated that although Rwanda's exports increased slightly from 1.8 percent in 1995 to 2.0 percent in 2015, the exports remain much lower than in the rest of sub-Saharan Africa (SSA). Exports in SSA account on average for 11 percent versus Rwanda's 2 percent. The same report showed that Rwanda's international trade – besides minerals and agricultural products that are exported to overseas markets – "is extremely concentrated by trading destination and goes almost exclusively to a few neighboring countries."[186] Further, Rwanda runs a trading deficit with its larger neighboring economies of Uganda and Kenya. And so, it came as a surprise on February 27, 2019, when Kagame suddenly closed Rwanda's main gateway to regional and global markets at Gatuna, the shared border with Uganda. Gatuna is Rwanda's busiest border, handling most of the country's international trade since most imports and exports pass through Uganda onto the seaport of Mombasa, Kenya. Kagame initially claimed on March 9, 2019, that

---

[186] Garth Frazer and Johannes Van Biesebroeck, "The Extent of Engagement in Global Value Chains by Firms in Rwanda," Op. Cit.

Gatuna's closure was due to infrastructure repairs and that the border would shortly reopen.[187] Kagame changed his story on March 25, 2019, explaining his decision to close Gatuna as follows:

> "The problem is not the road, or the road being constructed. The problem is politics. We have 100s of people from Rwanda, arrested, detained in prisons for years in Uganda, without being charged or appearing anywhere in court."[188]

To understand the insanity of closing the international border at Gatuna, let us take a closer look at the Rwanda trade with Uganda, Kenya, and the rest of the world. As shown in table 12, in 2017, Uganda's exports to Rwanda were worth US$182 million. Rwandan exports to Uganda were valued at US$9.8 million. The total trade between the two countries was, therefore, US$191 million.[189]

Table 12. Rwanda's international trade, 2017 (US$)

Trading partner	Rwanda's exports	Rwanda's imports (US$)	Total trade
Kenya	US$ 16.2 million	US$165 million	US$181.1 million
Uganda	US$9.8 million	US$182 million	US$191.1 million
International	US$948 million	US$2.2 billion	US$3.1 billion

Sources: Rwanda National Bank and World Bank data, 2017

---

[187] Remarks by President Kagame at the 16th National Leadership Retreat, Gabiro, 9 March 2019, https://www.youtube.com/watch?v=t2vSLlECUAk

[188] President Paul Kagame in a speech at CEO Forum, Kigali, Rwanda, March 25, 2019, https://twitter.com/urugwirovillage/status/1110109763038265345?s=21.

[189] World Bank, "Uganda exports, imports and trade balance By Country 2017," https://wits.worldbank.org/CountryProfile/en/Country/UGA/Year/2017/TradeFlow/EXPIMP/Partner/by-country

Rwanda's trade with Kenya, which transits through Uganda, comprised of Kenya's exports of US\$165 million and Rwandan exports of US\$16.2 million. The total trade between the two countries was US\$181 million. The total trade between Kenya, Rwanda, and Uganda is US\$372 million.[190] Clearly, Rwanda is a junior trading partner to both and Uganda and Kenya. Meanwhile, most of Rwanda's annual international trade, amounting to US\$3.1 billion, passes through Uganda into Kenya's seaport of Mombasa.[191] The importance of Gatuna in regional and international trade notwithstanding, Kagame ordered the Rwanda-Uganda border shut. Henceforth, Rwandans were not permitted to cross the border into Uganda and, by extension, to Kenya. Ugandan foreign minister Sam Kutesa described Rwanda's restrictions on the movement of goods and Rwandan citizens from Rwanda to Uganda as trade embargo:

> "On 28th February 2019, the Government of Rwanda
> decided to close its Katuna border with Uganda. Katuna
> is a One Stop Border Post. The Government of Rwanda
> also issued an advisory against travel of its nationals
> to Uganda … Export of Ugandan goods to Rwanda
> has been prohibited by Rwandan authorities. The same
> authorities have introduced an export permit system for
> people that intend to export goods to Uganda, which

---

[190] World Bank, "Kenya exports, imports and trade balance By Country and Region 2017, https://wits.worldbank.org/CountryProfile/en/Country/KEN/Year/2017/TradeFlow/EXPIMP

[191] See National Bank of Rwanda, External Trade Data, imports, 2017, https://www.bnr.rw/browse-in/statistics/external-sector-statistics/?tx_bnr documentmanager_frontend%5Bdocument%5D=237&tx_bnrdocumentmanager_ frontend%5Baction%5D=download&tx_bnrdocumentmanager_frontend %5Bcontroller%5D=Document&cHash=8125a38d5e7c71012c3b6065e9ed8cf6. For imports in 2017, see https://www.bnr.rw/browse-in/statistics/external-sector-statistics/?tx_bnrdocumentmanager_frontend%5Bdocument%5D=236&tx_ bnrdocumentmanager_frontend%5Baction%5D=download&tx_ bnrdocumentmanager_frontend%5Bcontroller%5D=Document&cHash= 1be27e50e815333f999e46cfca79176a.

is practically impossible to obtain. I have previously described this as a trade embargo, which indeed it is."[192]

Rwanda's export agency, the National Agricultural Export Development Board (NAEB), provides an insight into the self-inflicted harm caused by border closer. In its June 2019 *Export and Re-export Report*, NAEB indicated severe export decreases due to, among other things, "political climates in neighboring countries":

"During this month of June 2019, total export revenues were $34,447,243 compared to $54,576,596 in 2018 the same period, representing a decrease of 40.55%. The decrease was a result of drop in unit prices of traditional crops Tea and Coffee due to international prices … [and] due to non-tariff barriers and political climates in neighboring countries. The cumulative achievement from January to June 2019 revenues was $220,836,562 against $275,074,880 same period of 2018 representing a decrease of 20%."[193]

The impact of border closure was especially severe on Rwanda's dairy exports into the East African community as shown in Table 13. The exports of dairy products plummeted by 80 percent in the first quarter of 2019 for which statistics were available at the time of writing this work.

---

[192] Republic of Uganda, "Statement By Hon. Sam Kutesa Minister of Foreign Affairs at the Briefing to the Diplomatic Corps on the Status of The Uganda-Rwanda Relations 17th May 2019," https://www.mofa.go.ug/files/downloads/STATEMENT%20BY%20MFA%20AT%20THE%20BRIEFING%20TO%20THE%20DIPLOMATIC%20CORPS%20ON%20%20THE%20STATUS%20OF%20THE%20UGANDA%20.pdf

[193] Republic of Rwanda, National Agricultural Export Development Board, "June 2019 Report of Exports and Reexports", July 2019, retrieved September 19, 2019, https://naeb.gov.rw/fileadmin/Reports-Monthly/June%202019%20Report.pdf

Table 13: Dairy exports decline after Rwanda closed Uganda Border, February 2019

Month	Value of exports in 2018 (US$)	Value of exports in 2019	Decrease in exports (%)
February	386,079	664,452	
March	3,100,824	512,909	83.4
April	2,626,348	331,209	87.3
May	3,029,711	533,271	82.4
June	3,843,025	631,810	83.5

Source: National Agricultural Export Development Board

The Rwanda government newspaper *The New Times* decried the sharp decrease in export earnings, quoting James Biseruka, the managing director of the ruling party's business empire, CVL's Inyange Industries Ltd: "The decrease of Rwanda's dairy exports was partly attributed to losing Rwanda's dairy market in Uganda and Kenya. A lot of milk was being exported to Uganda and Kenya as they accounted for about 90 percent of milk export."[194] The National Institute for Statistics of Rwanda also reported that "Rwanda's re-exports to EAC partner states decreased by 33.74 percent in value terms during the first quarter of 2019 compared to the same quarter of 2018."[195]

The border closure has been especially devastating for small business in Rwanda, as *The East African* investigative report on Rwanda's

---

[194] Emmanuel Ntirenganya, "Agricultural exports drop by 9 percent", *The New Times*, September 15, 2019, https://www.newtimes.co.rw/news/agricultural-exports-drop-9-cent; See also Emmanuel Ntirenganya, "Agricultural exports drop by 9 percent", September 19, https://allafrica.com/stories/201909160075.html

[195] Republic of Rwanda, National Institute of Statistics of Rwanda, "Formal External Trade in Goods First Quarter 2019," June 2019, file:///C:/Users/David/Downloads/2019Q1%20External%20Trade%20Report.pdf

cross-border bus companies showed.[196] The report shows that Rwandan transport companies servicing the Rwanda-Uganda–Kenya route were devastated. Trinity Express, a Kigali-based bus company with more than ten buses, now deploys only one bus on the Kigali–Kampala route. Only foreign nationals, not Rwandans, use Trinity Express services. Previously, the company did more than twenty trips a day. Now, it can manage only one trip a day. Simba Coach, which travelled the Kigali–Nairobi via Kampala route, suspended three of its seven buses on the route. Rwandan bus companies were now essentially limited to carrying foreign travelers as Rwandans were trapped inside Rwanda.

Rwandan border closure provides another important insight, namely, how Rwanda routinely manipulates economic statistics. On September 14, 2019, Kagame announced that Rwanda's GDP grew by 8.4 percent in the first quarter and by 12.2 percent in the second quarter of 2019, declaring that few countries anywhere in the world can achieve this.[197] Kagame based his declarations on the data from the National Institute of Statistics of Rwanda, which maintained that agriculture expanded by 28 percent, industry by 17 percent, and services by 47 percent, which together contributed to a 12.2 percent GDP growth rate in the second quarter of 2019.[198]

The contribution by the agriculture sector to the tune of 28 percent cannot be believed. This is shown by the data of the National Bank of Rwanda and the National Agricultural Export Development Board, both of which declared poor performance by the agriculture and animal husbandry sector in the first and second quarter of 2019 compared to

---

[196] Johnson Kanamugire, "The Uganda-Rwanda border bus operators withdraw their fleet," The East African, May 9, 2019, http://rwandatoday.africa/news/Uganda-Rwanda-border-bus-operators-withdraw-their-fleet/4383214-5106234-rdsi1n/index.html

[197] President Paul Kagame, "President Kagame chairs RPF political bureau meeting," September 14, 2019, https://youtu.be/904D9w8kiPU

[198] Republic of Rwanda, National Institute of Statistics of Rwanda, "Gross Domestic Product Second Quarter 2019," retrieved September 21, 2019, file:///C:/Users/David/Downloads/R_GDP%20National%20Accounts%202019Q2_webnote_final.pdf

the previous year. As shown in Table 14, tea, which is Rwanda's main agricultural export did poorly, with its earnings plummeting by 13.2 percent from US$59.2 million in January-July 2018 to US$51.4 million in January-July 2019.[199] The decline in Rwanda's dairy industry was even more catastrophic, dipping by 79.1 percent from US$3.8 million in January-July 2018 to US$691,160 in January-July 2019.

Table 14. Agriculture and animal husbandry exports in first-second quarter of 2019 compared to 2018

Product	Value of exports, 2018 (US$)	Value of exports, 2019	Difference (%)
Coffee	28,272,854	26,435,196	7%
Tea	59,292,118	51,464,661	-13.2%
Hides and skins	4,737,069	2,238,985	-52.7%
Milk and milk products	3,843,025	691,160	-79.1%

Source: National Bank of Rwanda

According to the National Agricultural Export Development Board, the earnings from agricultural exports from January to June 2019 were US$220.8 million compared to US$275 in the period of 2018—a decrease of 20 percent.[200] The NAEB gives four reasons for the poor performance by the agriculture and animal husbandry sector during the first and second quarter of 2019. First, international prices for Rwanda's traditional cash crops of tea and coffee dropped. Second, "from January 2019 the registered reduction in rainfall affected subsequent months in terms of green leaf production. This had a negative impact on the

---

[199] Republic of Rwanda, National Bank of Rwanda, "Monthly Exports Period: July 2019," file:///C:/Users/David/Downloads/FORMAL MONTHLY EXPORTS 2019.pdf

[200] Republic of Rwanda, National Agricultural Export Development Board, "June 2019 Report of Exports and Reexports", July 2019, retrieved September 19, 2019, https://naeb.gov.rw/fileadmin/Reports-Monthly/June%202019%20Report.pdf

total production of the second semester where production reduced by 2,260,014Kgs representing (3%) of last year same period performance."[201] Third, the non-tariff barriers negatively affected exports. Fourth, the "political climates in neighboring countries" became a factor.[202] The question then is this: How could the agriculture and animal husbandry sector that was affected by poor rains, a drop in international prices, non-tariff barriers, and closure of the Rwanda-Uganda border, became the second-largest contributor to GDP growth in the second quarter of 2019?

The answer is simple. This is a case of statistical manipulation. And in this case, the doctoring of the data was done rather poorly. The government overlooked or forgot to harmonize three different institutions that gather and disseminate statistics. While the National Institute of Statistics of Rwanda and Kagame were proclaiming spectacular results in agriculture and animal husbandry, the National Bank of Rwanda and the National Agricultural Export Development Board were declaring the sector a poor performer affected by domestic and external factors.

A year before the border closure episode, Rwanda had engaged in a trade war with the US, which led to Rwanda's suspension from The African Growth and Opportunity Act (AGOA). Enacted in 2000, AGOA enhances market access to the US for qualifying sub-Saharan African countries, including Rwanda. In order to qualify for AGOA trade benefits, SSA countries must meet statutory eligibility requirements, including making progress toward establishing market-based economies, the rule of law, political pluralism, and elimination of barriers to American investment and trade. In 2015, the East African Community launched a plan to ban imports of used clothing and footwear by 2019. When challenged by the US under AGOA rules of

---

[201] Republic of Rwanda, National Agricultural Export Development Board, "June 2019 Report of Exports and Reexports", Ibid.

[202] Republic of Rwanda, National Agricultural Export Development Board, "June 2019 Report of Exports and Reexports", Ibid.

open markets, the three major AGOA beneficiaries in the region that actively export into the US—Kenya, Tanzania, and Uganda—worked with American authorities to implement a formula that satisfied all the parties. Kenya, Tanzania, and Uganda continued to receive full OGOA benefits. Rwanda refused to negotiate, insisting on keeping a policy that raised tariffs on imports of used apparel and footwear by over 1,000 percent, effectively banning imports of these products. On July 30, 2018, the United States suspended Rwanda from AGOA. As explained by the Deputy United States Trade Representative C.J. Mahoney,

> "President Donald J. Trump issued a proclamation regarding Rwanda that enforces the eligibility criteria established by Congress for trade preferences under the African Growth and Opportunity Act (AGOA). This proclamation suspends the application of duty-free treatment for all apparel products from Rwanda. We regret this outcome and hope it is temporary. But if the AGOA eligibility criteria are to have any meaning, they have to be enforced—particularly where, as here, other AGOA members took action in order remain in compliance. The President's action today is measured and proportional."[203]

For a country purportedly marching towards an upper-middle-income and high-income economy that is integrated into regional and global markets, Kagame's Rwanda was moving in the opposite direction—on the road to a pariah state isolated from both regional and global markets.

---

[203] US Trade Representative, "President Donald J. Trump Upholds AGOA Trade Preference Eligibility Criteria with Rwanda," July 30, 2018, https://ustr.gov/about-us/policy-offices/press-office/press-releases/2018/july/president-donald-j-trump-upholds-agoa

The Failure of Kagame's Faustian Bargain

Since launching Rwanda Vision 2020 for transforming Rwanda into a middle-income economy, Paul Kagame has accumulated enormous powers and influence at home and abroad. During his tenure, which has taken various forms since 1994, Rwanda became essentially a single-party state, dominated by the Rwandan Patriotic Front, which became synonymous with Kagame in the role of unreplaceable benevolent strongman that dominates both politics and economics. Jetting around the world in his presidential Gulfstream G650 to Ivy League graduations for his children, debating the global elites at Davos, lecturing at Harvard Business School, and giving keynote speeches at the World Bank, Kagame became easily Africa's most successful autocrat. The basis of this lifestyle was the 2003 constitution, which granted Kagame two terms of seven years each, which was amended in 2015 to allow him to stay in power up to 2034. In the elections of 2017, he won by 99 percent, after imprisoning his competitors. Besides immunizing him from prosecution for any crimes when he leaves office, the current constitution grants him powers to appoint and dismiss senior public servants in the three branches of government, including the chief justice and the president of the senate.

With these powers, Kagame tolerates no opposition and pursues his political opponents wherever they may be, leading to accusations of repression at home and abroad. The United Nations DR Congo Mapping Report concluded, for example, that "the apparent systematic and widespread attacks" unleashed by Rwandan armies in Congo "reveal a number of inculpatory elements that, if proven before a competent court, could be characterized as crimes of genocide."[204] In the realm of economics, Kagame and his RPF built a business empire that became Rwanda's largest investment group that thrives on government contracts, while the competitors saw their companies seized under all manner of pretexts. Crony capitalism is the name of the game in Rwanda.

Kagame's cunningly branded himself a technocrat and successfully built a powerful global lobby that championed him as a visionary leader creating wealth and improving Rwandan lives. The donors that detested Kagame's heavy-handedness saw him as dictator who at least got things done. But, as argued in this book, Kagame struck a Faustian bargain—he was willing to sacrifice anything to satisfy a limitless thirst for power, astutely convincing the world to look the other way whenever he unleashed violence at home or abroad, because, after all, he improved the lives of fellow Rwandans. As in the legend of Faust, Kagame delivered neither the human rights nor transformed the lives of the people of Rwanda, who remain among the world's poorest.

For foreign aid givers, this was not first time they have made a terrible mistake in Rwanda. When from 1973 to 1994 Rwanda was led by another military dictator, General Juvénal Habyarimana, the donors were impressed by his advances in agriculture, education, health, and industry. The World Bank was particularly impressed with Rwanda's GDP growth rates under Habyarimana—the single indicator was said to demonstrate effective development performance. This is how,

---

[204] UN High Commission for Human Rights, "Democratic Republic of The Congo, 1993–2003 Report of the Mapping Exercise documenting the most serious violations of human rights and international humanitarian law committed within the territory of the Democratic Republic of the Congo between March 1993 and June 2003," August 2010, https://www.ohchr.org/Documents/Countries/CD/DRC_MAPPING_REPORT_FINAL_EN.pdf

in 1986, the World Bank described the Habyarimana government's socioeconomic performance:

> "Rwanda has attempted with a large measure of success to satisfy its subsistence needs and to make important advances in agriculture, education, health and small-scale industry. These achievements have been facilitated by the cultural and social cohesion of its people, political stability, and overall sound economic management. During the period of 1977-82, the rate of growth of GDP, in real terms, averaged about five percent per annum, reflecting sustained good performance by most sectors."[205]

Four years after the World Bank glorified Rwanda as a country with cultural and social cohesion among its people, political stability, and overall sound economic management, the country went up in flames ending in genocide in 1994. The next Rwandan military ruler, General Paul Kagame, was to receive the exact same donor compliments. Here is the World Bank describing the accomplishment of the Kagame regime in 2018:

> "Rwanda has made extraordinary progress in recent years. It is one of the few countries anywhere in the world that has managed a "triple crown" of fast economic growth, robust reductions in poverty, and a narrowing of inequality. The poverty rate fell from 59 percent to 45 percent in the last decade and Rwanda is

---

[205] The World Bank, "Staff Appraisal Report," Rwandese Republic, March 19, 1986, http://documents.worldbank.org/curated/en/503491468305093064/pdf/multi-page.pdf

now ranked as the second easiest place to do business in all of Africa."[206]

There are signs, however, that Kagame will face greater scrutiny in the coming years. His international support has disintegrated. The Clintons and the Blairs do not have as much influence in the corridors of power in the United States and Britain. Perhaps the biggest loss for Kagame has been the departure of Jim Yong Kim from the World Bank. We can already see the changed environment in the World Bank, illustrated by its *Rwanda Systematic Diagnostic Report*, 2019 and *Rwanda Energy Access Diagnostic Report*, 2019. The diagnostic reports peel off the layers of delusional grandeur sector by sector and concludes that Rwanda Vision 2020 and the envisaged prize of reaching a middle-income economy is dead in the water. Post–Jim Yong Kim World Bank may be following in the footsteps of the World Economic Forum (WEF) in freeing itself from Kagame's propaganda. WEF appears to have had serious second thoughts about the Kagame economic miracle—the global think tank dropped Rwanda from the fifty-second ranking in the 2016[207] global competitiveness report to 108th position in 2018.[208] Without an explanation, sub-Saharan countries of Seychelles, South Africa, Botswana, Kenya, Namibia, and Ghana were reclassified together with Mauritius ahead of Rwanda as should be the case given that Rwanda is comparatively an economic dwarf.

---

[206] The World Bank, "New World Bank Group Development Strategy Will Help Rwanda Create Jobs, Boost Agricultural Productivity and Spur Private Sector Investments," 2014-2018, https://www.worldbank.org/en/country/rwanda/publication/new-world-bank-group-development-strategy-will-help-rwanda-create-jobs-boost-agricultural-productivity-and-spur-private-sector-investments

[207] Word Economic Forum, "The Global Competitiveness Report 2016," http://www3.weforum.org/docs/GCR2016-2017/05FullReport/TheGlobalCompetitivenessReport2016-2017_FINAL.pdf

[208] Word Economic Forum, "The Global Competitiveness Report 2018," http://www3.weforum.org/docs/GCR2018/05FullReport/TheGlobalCompetitivenessReport2018.pdf

The equation has also changed in Africa. When Kagame closed the common border with Uganda in February 2019, he dug himself in a deep hole from which he was unable to climb out of at the time of writing. Half of Rwandan international trade goes through Uganda onto the Kenyan seaport of Mombasa, while Uganda and Kenya are the main Rwandan trading partners. Rwandan neighbors ignored Kagame, who happened to be the chairman of the East African Community, which includes Uganda. Further to the south, a court in South Africa indicted what it determined were the Kagame government's associates, who assassinated the exiled former Rwandan intelligence chief, Patrick Karegeya. At the time of writing, South African National Prosecuting Authority had issued arrest warrants for the implicated Rwandan assassins, and the Kagame government had yet to respond.[209] The South African case marked the first time a foreign government tied a killing to the Kagame government and followed up with prosecutorial action, unlike other countries, where diaspora Rwandans mysteriously die and host governments take no action.

---

[209] Michela Wrong, "South Africa Asks Rwanda to Hand Over Karegeya Murder Suspects," Guardian, September 9, 2019, https://www.theguardian.com/world/2019/sep/09/south-africa-asks-rwanda-to-hand-over-karegeya-suspects

BIBLIOGRAPHY

The primary sources for this book come from the government of Rwanda. The next major primary sources are official reports of donor agencies and donor countries that work closely with Rwanda, including the World Bank and the International Monetary Fund. In the third category are the Clinton and Blair foundations, followed by media reports. The bibliography is organized in that order.

Official Reports of the Government of Rwanda

Auditor General, Report of The Auditor General of State Finances for the Year Ended 30 June 2018.

Auditor General, Report of The Auditor General of State Finances for the Year Ended 30 June 2017.

Claver Gatete, Minister of Finance, The Rwanda We Want: Towards Vision 2050, December 16, 2016.

Energy Utility Corporation Ltd, Annual Report and Financial Statements for the Year Ended 30 June 2018.

Ministry of Education, 2018 Education Statistics, December 2018.

Ministry of Finance and Economic Planning, Comment by Minister of Finance to Rwanda mention in Panama Papers, 6 April 2016.

Ministry of Finance and Economic Planning, Rwanda's $400 million Eurobond named 2013 Deal of the Year by Euromoney, February 25, 2014.

Ministry of Health, Report of Development of Rwanda Master Facility List, Final Report, November 2018.

Ministry of Infrastructure, National Sanitation Policy, December 2016.

Ministry of Infrastructure, Water and Sanitation Sector Strategic Plan 2013/14 -2017/18, June 2013.

National Agricultural Export Development Board, June 2019 Report of Exports and Re-exports, July 2019.

National Institute of Statistics of Rwanda, Gross Domestic Product Second Quarter 2019, September 2019.

National Institute of Statistics of Rwanda, Labor Force Survey Annual Report, December 2018.

Parliament of Rwanda, Constitution of the Republic of Rwanda, 2015.

Rwanda Commercial High Court, Société Pétrolière sarl (SP) C/ Bakri International Energy Co (Rwanda) Ltd (Bakri Rwanda) R COM A 0214/10/HCC 04/08/2010.

Rwanda Development Board, Rwanda Development Board registers over US$2 billion worth of investments in 2018, January 8, 2019.

Rwanda Energy Group, Rwanda Least Cost Power Development Plan (LCPDP) 2019—2040, June 2019.

Rwanda Environment Management Authority, State of Environment and Outlook Report 2017.

Rwanda Revenue Authority, Annual Activity Report 2017/18, October 2018

Rwanda Transport Development Agency, Annual Report Fiscal Year 2017/2018.

Official Reports of Donor Agencies and Donor Countries

African Development Bank

Rwanda and African Development Bank sign €229 million loan agreements to finance electricity projects, October 17, 2018.

European Union

European Union-Republic of Rwanda National Indicative Program for the Period 2014-2020, 2014.

International Monetary Fund

Rwanda: Ninth Review Under the Policy Support Instrument, May 23, 2018.

Rwanda: Sixth Review Under the Three-Year Arrangement Under the Poverty Reduction and Growth Facility (PRGF), Requests for Waivers of Non-observance of Performance Criteria, July 2006.

Rwanda: Staff Report for the 2019 Article IV Consultation and Request for A Three-Year Policy Coordination Instrument, July 2019.

Rwanda: Tenth Review Under the Policy Support Instrument, November 2018.

Statement by IMF Managing Director Christine Lagarde at the Conclusion of a Visit to Rwanda, January 29, 2015.

United Kingdom Government

David Cameron, Engagements Oral Answers to Questions, Prime Minister in the House of

Commons at 11:30 am on 17th October 2012.

DIFID does not give any money to Rwandan sponsorship of Arsenal FC, May 27, 2018.

Visit Rwanda's sponsorship of Arsenal FC, June 11, 2018.

DFID Rwanda Profile, Planned Budget for 2018/2019 and 2019/2020, July 2018.

United States Government

Department of Justice, Foreign Agents Registration by W2 Group Inc on Master Service Agreement by and between Government of Rwanda and W2 Group, Inc., August 12, 2011.

Department of Justice, Rwanda 2018 Human Rights Report, 2019.

Embassy, Rwanda, Charge Cheryl Sim, Chevron Pulls Out of Rwanda, August 13, 2008.

Department of State, 2019 Investment Climate Statements: Rwanda, July 11, 2019.

Office of US Trade Representative, President Donald J. Trump Upholds AGOA Trade Preference Eligibility Criteria with Rwanda, July 30, 2018.

Treasury Department, Dr Jim Kim meeting with Rwandan president Paul Kagame, March 23, 2012.

White House, Early Reactions to the Nomination of Jim Yong Kim as President of the World Bank, March 23, 2012

World Bank Group

Doing Business 2019, May 19, 2019.

Future Drivers of Rwanda, 2019.

Human Capital Index: Country Briefs and Data, 2018.

Jim Yong Kim's Remarks, President Kagame receives World Bank Group President, March 22, 2017.

Jim Yong Kim, Remarks, World Bank Group President Jim Yong Kim at the 2018 Annual Meetings Plenary, October 12, 2018.

Kristalina Georgieva, Speech made after the launch of Rwanda's The Future Drivers of Growth Report, December 18, 2018.

Lighting Rwanda: Rwanda Economic Update, June 2019.

New World Bank Group Development Strategy Will Help Rwanda Create Jobs, Boost Agricultural Productivity and Spur Private Sector Investments, 2014-2018, 2014.

Project Appraisal Document on a Proposed Credit in the Amount of SDR 145.2 Million (US$200 Million) to the Republic of Rwanda for the Rwanda Quality Basic Education for Human Capital Development Project, July 9, 2019.

Rwanda Energy Sector Development Policy Loan, March 20, 2017.

Rwanda: Energy Access Diagnostic Report Based on the Multi-Tier Framework, June 2018.

Rwanda: Systematic Country Diagnostic Report, June 25, 2019.

Rwanda Priority Skills for Growth (PSG) (P252350), Archived September 28, 2018.

Rwanda Electricity Access Scale-up Project (P111567), March 30, 2018.

Robert Zoellick, World Bank President Praises Rwanda's Energy Sector, August 12, 2009.

Second Rwanda Energy Sector Development Policy Financing, October 19, 2018.

Second Rwanda Energy Sector Development Policy Financing (P166458), May-2018.

Staff Appraisal Report, Rwandese Republic, March 19, 1986.

Sub-Saharan Africa Macro Poverty Outlook, Springs Meeting 2019.

Tackling Stunting: An Unfinished Agenda, Rwanda Economic Update, June 2018.

Transcript: "Delivering Results—A Conversation with Jim Yong Kim, Tony Blair, and Michael Barber," April 10, 2013.

Understanding the Africa country policy and institutional assessment (CPIA) 2017, September 12, 2018.

World Bank Announces Open Access Policy for Research and Knowledge, Launches Open Knowledge Repository, April 10, 2012.

World Food Programme, National Institute of Statistics of Rwanda, and Ministry of Agriculture and Animal Resources, and "Rwanda 2018 | Comprehensive food security and vulnerability analysis," December 2018.

Reports of the Foundations

Clinton Foundation

Clinton, 20 minutes with Bill Clinton - up against 'big poppa', BBC Interview, August 12, 2013.

Clinton Health Access Initiative, Inc., Cumulative Donations by Donor (January 2010 to March 2019)," Retrieved on August 22, 2019.

Clinton, speaking on achievements of Rwanda across all sectors and commits to assisting Rwanda's health sector in becoming free from foreign aid through partnership between the Ministry of Health, Clinton Initiative and 13 top US schools, YouTube, published on July 20, 2012.

Jim Yong Kim, President of the World Bank, How the Clinton Global Initiative Changed the Way Wealth is Put to Work, Remarks delivered at the Clinton Global Initiative's 12th and final Annual Meeting, *published on Medium by the Clinton Foundation, January 10, 2017.*

Tony Blair Africa Governance Initiative

Gatsby Charitable Foundation, Rwanda Government - We supported the Tony Blair Africa Governance Initiative to help build the capacity and functioning of institutions at the centre of the Rwandan Government, retrieved August 28, 2019.

The Tony Blair Africa Governance Initiative, Annual Report and Financial Statement, February 28, 2017.

Tony Blair hailed President Kagame's visionary leadership as he saw for himself the remarkable pace of Rwandan progress during a two-day visit to the East African country, Africa Governance Initiative announcement, November 16, 2009.

Tony Blair Africa Governance Initiative, Our mission is to make government work for the world's poorest people, retrieved August 26, 2019.

Media Reports

Musoni, Edwin, "Kagame unveils model granite factory," The New Times, July 7, 2012.

Byaruhanga, Catherine, "How the Rwanda-Uganda border crossing came to a halt," BBC Africa, 9 March 2019.

Collins, David, Cherie Blair helps get bail for Rwandan spy chief fighting extradition to Spain over alleged war crimes, *Mirror*, June 24, 2015.

Cordery, Stacy, "In retirement, most ex-presidents can't resist the urge to stay relevant", *The Conversation*, June 20, 2018.

Dartmouth College Press Release, "US Partners with Rwanda to Dramatically Expand Health Workforce Dartmouth Among Leading Medical Institutions Bridging Human Resource Gaps," November 20, 2013.

De Wet Potgierter and Raymond Joseph, "Rwanda splurges on luxury jets," *Sunday Times*, February 14, 2010.

Economist, Party of Business: The Rwandan Patriotic Front Business Empire, *March 2, 2017.*

Hakim, Danny, "Tony Blair Has Used His Connections to Change the World, and to Get Rich," *The New York Times*, August 5, 2014.

Harding, Robin, "World Bank: Man on mission—an ambitious restructuring program by Jim Yong Kim, Bank President, has attracted both admiration and criticism—but can it deliver?" Financial Times, April 7, 2014.

Himbara, David, "RwandAir Bankrupting Rwanda—Open Letter to Presidents Yoweri Museveni and John Magufuli," Medium.com, May 17, 2018.

International Consortium of Investigative Journalists, "Rwanda: Emmanuel Ndahiro, Brigadier General (2015-present); Chief of the intelligence agency in Rwanda (2004-2011)", *Panama Papers*.

Kagame, Paul, "Rwanda and the new lions of Africa," *Wall Street Journal*, May 19, 2013.

Kanamugire, Johnson, "The Uganda-Rwanda border bus operators withdraw their fleet," *The East African*, May 9, 2019.

Kimenyi, Bryan, "Kagame launches Kigali Convention Centre", The New Times, July 8, 2016.

Linskey, Annie, "State Dept. aided Clinton-backed Rwanda effort: Bill Clinton wanted to build a new health system in Rwanda. His wife's State Department delivered big time," *Boston Globe*, October 17, 2015.

McGreal, Chris, "Tony Blair defends support for Rwandan leader Paul Kagame," *The Guardian*, December 31, 2010.

Mendick, Robert, "Cherie Blair's empire and its secret HQ, The wife of the former prime minister is enjoying her most successful year yet as her law firm and charity both pick up contracts around the world," *The Telegraph*, March 14, 2014

Michel, Louis, "Rwanda's track record on MDGs should inspire others", EURACTIV.COM, Sept 26, 2013.

Nsehe, <u>Mfonobong</u>, "Rwandan Tobacco Millionaire Tribert Rujugiro Loses Shopping Mall to Government," *Forbes*, September 29, 2017.

Emmanuel Ntirenganya, "Agricultural exports drop by 9 percent", *The New Times*, September 15, 2019.

Sack, Kevin and Fink, Sheri, "Rwanda Aid Shows Reach and Limits of Clinton Foundation: In addition to doing goods, the foundation enhances the Clinton brand, never more than while Hillary Rodham Clinton is running for president," *The New York Times*, October 18, 2015.

Savchuk, Katia, How Rwanda went from genocide to global health model, *Global Post*, April 8, 2014.

Seelye, Katharine, "And for My Second Act, I'll Make Some Money", *The New York Times*, September 9, 2007.

Wallis, William, *Financial Times*, "Rwandan Patriotic Front: Party builds a formidable business," September 24, 2012.

White, Michael, "The former British PM is trousering millions of pounds from the international lecture circuit", The Guardian, April 10, 2009.

Wrong, Michela, "South Africa Asks Rwanda to Hand Over Karegeya Murder Suspects," The Guardian, September 9, 2019.

Yoon, Robert, "$153 million in Bill and Hillary Clinton speaking fees, documented", *CNN*, February 6, 2016.

www.ingramcontent.com/pod-product-compliance
Lightning Source LLC
Chambersburg PA
CBHW051459250726
48655CB00001B/501